AF227968

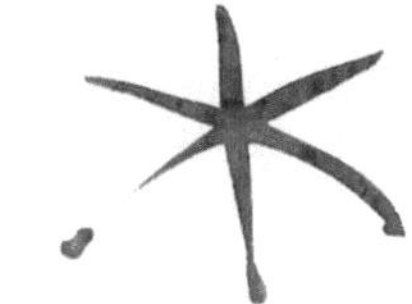

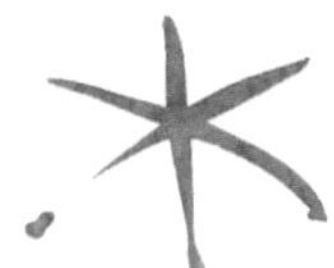

Aster(ix) Journal
www.asterixjournal.com

Editor-in-chief/Founder
Angie Cruz

Publisher/Founder
Adriana E. Ramírez

Managing Editor
Tanya Shirazi

Editorial Assistants
Clarissa León
Joshua Graber
Katherinna Mar

Book Review Editor
Lucia LoTempio

Contributing Editors
Rosa Alcalá, Arielle Greenberg, Yona Harvey, Daisy Hernandez, J. A. Howard, Sheila Maldonado, Dawn Lundy Martin, Oindrila Mukherjee, Idra Novey, Emily Raboteau, Nelly Rosario, Zohra Saed, Sun Yung Shin, Jenelle Troxell, Chika Unigwe, Marta Lucía Vargas, Autumn Womack, Elleni Centime Zeleke

Advisory Editors
Ari Ariel, Armando Garcia, Amy Sara Carroll, Norma Cantú, Xochi Candalaria, Jennifer Clement, Edwidge Danticat, Cristina García, Stephanie Elizondo Griest, Andrea Thome, Helena Maria Viramontes

Aster(ix) print issues are usually published 2-3 times a year in print with additional content online. **Aster(ix)** is funded in part by the Dietrich School of Arts and Sciences and the Department of English at University of Pittsburgh.

More Aster(ix) Anthologies

The Poetry Issue
Winter 2020

Inheritance
Summer 2019

**(Un)bound
[double issue]**
Winter 2018/2019

Edges
Fall 2018

Dirty Laundry
Fall 2017

Kitchen Table Translation
Summer 2017

Best of Kweli
Spring 2017

What We Love
Fall 2016

Atravesando
Spring 2016

available for order wherever books are sold

and don't forget to visit
asterixjournal.com
for more content and information

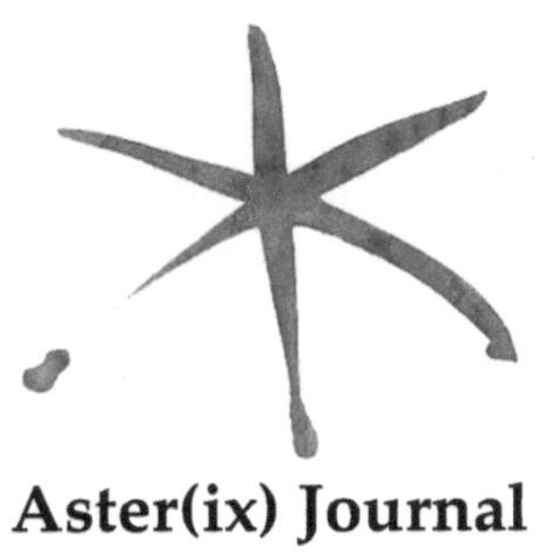

Aster(ix) Journal

presents

The Ferrante Project:
The Freedom of Anonymity

October 2020

BLUE SKETCH PRESS | PITTSBURGH

Published via Blue Sketch Press, Pittsburgh.
www.bluesketchpress.com

The Ferrante Project: The Freedom of Anonymity
An Aster(ix) Anthology / Aster(ix) Journal
1st ed.
      ISBN (print)   978-1-942547-13-6 (trade paperback)
                              1-942547-13-6 (ISBN-10)
Cover art by Amanda Tien
Cover Design by Little Owl Creative

First Edition: October 2020

Printed in the United States of America
9 8 7 6 5 4 3 2 1

For Adalis Martínez — Rest In Power

The contributors to *The Ferrante Project* include:
Cathy Linh Che, Angie Cruz, Natalie Díaz, Ru
Freeman, Sarah Gambito, Cristina García, Jamey
Hatley, Dawn Lundy Martin, Ayana Mathis, Vi khi
Nao, Aimee Nezhukumatathil, Deborah Paredez,
Khadijah Queen, Emily Raboteau, Paisley Rekdal,
Lyrae Van Clief-Stefanon.

Contents

The Ferrante Project:
The Freedom of Anonymity
The Editors

We, the editors for *The Ferrante Project*, having finished a bottle of Mezcal in one of our kitchens, out of a burning desire to unshackle ourselves from the anxiety of notoriety, to restore a sense of play, to contraindicate the cult of personality, posturing, and preemptive celebrity at the expense (sometimes) of the quality and provocation of the work itself, hereby announce a collective.

Because we admire Elena Ferrante for her extreme excavation of previously unexplored material–female friendship–and also denounce the asshole who worked to expose her identity, the following questions arise for us: What is the benefit of being anonymous for a woman? What kind of freedom and possibility can writing anonymously offer to women writers, and in particular to women writers of color? Regarding anonymity, Ferrante said, "I simply decided once and for all...to liberate myself from the anxiety of notoriety...thanks to this decision, I have gained a space of my own, a space that is free, where I feel active and present."

The Ferrante Project: The freedom of anonymity, brings together sixteen women writers of color (alongside sixteen visual artists in a linked project with the Warhol Museum in Pittsburgh, Pennsylvania).

This inaugural literary issue brings women writers of color to anonymously contribute new works as an investment in possibility and the possibility for failure. Although most of us felt prompted by a need to step out of prescribed roles as mothers, professors, organizers, and spokeswomen to write liberated from expectations and duty, common themes in the work for this project include physical decline, menopause, mental health, resentment, and rage against patriarchy.

Though some of us disagreed about the accuracy of using the term "anonymity," when naming the members of the collective, the majority of us decided to do so in service of the project where working anonymously as a collective will create a productive and charged tension between the freedom of writing anonymously and the possibility of being discovered.

The Editors

The Ferrante Project is a collaboration between CAAPP: The Center for African American Poetry and Poetics and Aster(ix) Journal.

The Days of Relinquishment

What kind of freedom and possibility can writing anonymously offer to women writers, and in particular to women writers of color?

<u>Day 1</u>
Would I—at last—tell the truth?

<u>Day 2</u>
Or would I tell a lie, untie the knotted rope tethering me to the shore of my comfort, the lie—I tell myself—that leads to release?

<u>Day 3</u>
Is the veiled name closer to the one or the other?

<u>Day 4</u>
Would I—at last—speak only to other dark women?

<u>Day 5</u>
Adrienne Rich: *These notes are concerned with relationships between and among women.*

<u>Day 6</u>
Would I speak our true names? Would I even begin to know how?

Would I speak about how often our names show our color—Tamika or Nguyen or González—the shade under which our voices are cast? Would I speak about how often we go unnamed in our triumphs and in our deaths? Would I forsake my singular name so I can speak—at last—more truly our many names? Would I even begin to know how? Would I Say Her Name? Sandra? Or hers? Gabriella? Or hers? Saartjie? Soo Yun? Socorro?

Day 7

Elena Ferrante: *I had to start with myself and with my relationships with other women—this is another essential formula—if I really wanted to give myself a shape.*

Day 8

Would I dare to admit—at last—that most days I can't stand Beyoncé and the clomping-capitalist-clock baseline of her ordered rhythms?

Day 9

Would I write to another rhythm? With what would I keep time? Would I keep time? Would I let it go? Would I stop spending or losing or managing or wasting or making or maximizing it? Would I tell menstrual time? Would I write in blood? Would I write the blood? Would I tell it in bloodtime? Would I write and write and write until I could—at last—feel the bloodrush and find in it another way to name myself rather than through the accretion of accomplishment? Would I banish the words *popular prize-winning productive professor promotion publicity published*?

Day 10

Ferrante: *Honest writing forces itself to find words for those parts of our experience that are crouched and silent.*

Day 11
Would I write in the form of a quipu, those knotted cords the Incans used for recording memories, for marking the days? Would I make of each word a knot—an overhand, a slip, a figure-eight—clustered on colored threads that refuse easy deciphering?

Day 12
Would I talk about that night over dinner when, after two decades of friendship, X said to me in passing, *Well, you know, girl, how you hate white women?*

Day 13
Rich: *And so we must take seriously the question of truthfulness between women, truthfulness among women.*

Day 14
Would I ask myself why I feel compelled to speak in this way, propelled toward the confessional? Would I ask what has made me feel I must speak as if I've done something wrong?

Day 15
Would I write that I was shocked by what X said? Would I admit what I said to her later that night—what I thought was the truth explained—while I was lying in bed? *Well, girl, you know because I'm lighter than you, because in fleeting moments I can be mistaken as one of their own, because I let them assume their familiarity, these white girls are always showing me themselves and I guess I'm just sick of seeing it.*

Day 16
Rich: *In speaking of lies, we come inevitably to the subject of truth. . . . There*

is no "the truth," "a truth"—truth is not one thing or even a system. It is an increasing complexity. The pattern of the carpet is a surface. When we look closely, or when we become weavers, we learn of the tiny multiple threads unseen in the overall pattern, the knots on the underside of the carpet.

Day 17

Would I write until—at last—I settled into the knotted underside of my disdain for Beyoncé? Would I confess that when I look closely at it what I see is actually my own self-disgust for the ways I tie my aspirations, my self-assertion, my success, my sense of power or beauty to the marketplace? A double knot I kneel to tighten each day.

Day 18

Ferrante: *I prefer to think of myself as being inside a tangled knot; tangled knots fascinate me.*

Day 19

Would I say what I told X days after—the darker truth under the one light enough to float to the surface? *You know, I wonder if really I've been performing this "I hate white women routine" all these years so you won't leave me, so you'll know I'm on our side, so you'll believe I'm dark enough, so I'll believe it, so I can prove to us that I won't let my light-skinned privilege betray us.* Would I write what I didn't say after that? How I assumed— like only a light-skinned girl can—that I had to perform my color? Would I write how I was only just then seeing the betrayal I had already committed, how what I was really saying was, *I'm afraid of what I'm capable of, afraid that you will see how brittle I am, nothing but a moth's wing battering itself against the lampshade?*

Day 20

Rich: *What is this particular fear that possesses the liar? . . . She is afraid, not so much of prison guards or bosses, but of something unnamed within her.*

Day 21

Would I try to make of my writing something akin to Cecilia Vicuña's "Disappeared Quipu," an art installation that transformed an empty room into thick curtains of knotted wool? Would my writing entangle the body in a roomful of knots?

Day 22

Would I confess that, even still, I am trying to imagine a way to list this on my CV?

Day 23

Would I admit how even though I read all four of Ferrante's Neapolitan novels, I struggled to keep going, that I grew increasingly, irritatingly weary of how I felt they relished in the abjection of their female protagonists? Does this make me unwilling to see certain truths about the ties between two poor girls, one light-skinned and one dark? Does this make me someone who wants to transcend these truths? Does this make me someone who wants to speak only in knots?

Day 24

Would I concede that, yes, if I'm really being honest, I actually enjoyed the Destiny's Child reunion during Beyoncé's Coachella performance, especially when they sang, *If you're really being honest / If you really want this / Why you acting like a stranger / What's with your behavior / Say my name, say my name?*

Day 25

Would I cease—at last—writing my condemnations? Would I stop performing my derision in the name of incisive and dispassionate analysis and instead relinquish myself to love? Would I write about the dark folds of my mother's body? Or of my own mother-marked body? Would I—at last—narrate the body without despair, without the syntax of destiny, without a yearning for the smooth, taught, untangled thread?

Day 26
Is the knot the word or the silence?

Day 27
Would I confess that I loved how Beyoncé shared the stage at Coachella with all those HBCU bodies—the flexed arms of the drumline, the arched backs of baton twirlers, the nimble ankles of the steppers, the glistening thighs of drill team dancers, the gloriously dark music of their names—Simone Jenee Arnetta Venzella Jasmin Kiandra Kimmie Fulani Kendra Nirine Mao Elysandra Khadijah . . . ?

Day 28
Would I thread together every word I write into a love knot for X? For all the XXs glistening, listening in the dark?

Quoted material taken from:

Adrienne Rich, "Women and Honor: Some Notes on Lying," *On Lies, Secrets, and Silence: Selected Prose* (New York: W.W. Norton, 1979), 185–94.

Elissa Schappell, "The Mysterious Anonymous Author Elena Ferrante on the Conclusion of Her Neapolitan Novels," *Vanity Fair*, August 27, 2015 (https://www.vanityfair.com/culture/2015/08/elena-ferrante-interview-the-story-of-the-lost-child).

The Agreement

PROPERTY SETTLEMENT AGREEMENT

THE AGREEMENT dated the ___________day of _____________ ,
2019, by and between X, hereinafter referred to as "she/her,"

A

N

D

Y, hereinafter referred to as "he/him."

WITNESSETH THAT:

WHEREAS, the parties hereto were committed on a day when both X
and Y were in a crisis. A low point in their lives where events forced an
unlikely partnership.

X had fled from the Southwest to New York City to sober up from a
love addiction with a man who secretly had a vasectomy. Imagine the
feelings of betrayal. X, all her life, wanted children, to ensure the lineage
of X's mother's family that could be traced back hundreds of years, to a
time when the original colonizers had set foot on their land and ravaged
her community. Her great-great-great-great-grandmother was one of
the only survivors. It was X's responsibility to make sure no one forgot
what had happened to X's people. They will pay, is what X's family said

every night at dinner instead of prayer.

Y had been given one last chance by his hopeful and all-loving gallerist to prove Y's self as an artist in one of the most important art fairs in New York. His gallerist saw himself in Y. He, too, had grown up working-class and had had to charm his way into the bourgeoisie. He too had black behind the ears and had to cut himself off from all he knew to find acceptance in the art world that he discovered was funded by the fascists, inheritors of those who rounded up members of his own people and threw them in cages, investors of corrupt companies who in the end became rich by exploiting his community. For the gallerist, if Y succeeded, the compromises he had made to succeed would absolve him. For five solid years the gallerist wholeheartedly believed that it would just take one collector, one curator, one influential critic, one museum show, just one, to launch Y's career. Y was full of promise and potential. Y could surely play in the big leagues if only someone, anyone, would give him a chance. But when Y failed once again to sell any of his works at the Armory Show in New York, to offset the extraordinary investment the gallerist had made, the gallerist finally understood that he didn't have the power and influence to break Y out. The gallerist was deeply in debt. The patronage was over. Y was on his own, devastated and alone.

Oh, Witness, you've read enough stories to know that for a love addict like X, who had escaped to New York City to pull the nail out of her heart, she will undoubtedly grab another nail to replace it. Ache begets ache. And imagine Y and his heartbreak. The one person in the world who believed in Y had given up on him. X met Y when he understood he was doomed to failure. Even if many at the art fair had said again and again that Y's work was among the best of all the fair, not one of the collectors took a risk and bought Y's work. Instead he was given advice to consider that in today's art market it's best to make work that people want to post on Instagram. Something large, something that pops on a cell phone screen. Y's work was impossible to photograph, it had to be experienced. In fact, Y believed that it would take a great poet to convey how the heart is moved when in the vicinity of his masterpieces.

This is when it happens, the birth of something, when you thirst, when the belly growls, when the streets are bombed, when the walls come down, when the earth cracks open.

This is how X found Y, on a bench, in a park, near the art fair. Both devastated. Both heartbroken.

I must make art. I must make art, Y said repeatedly. What would the world be without art? Unbearable! It's all I know how to do.

I must make a baby. I must make a baby, said X. My ancestors will never forgive me if I fail at this.

WITNESSETH THAT:

WHEREAS, the parties have resolved that it is impossible to continue the relationship between them for *reasons known to them*, and X intends to file a Complaint of Divorce in the Court of Common Pleas.

Reasons known to them:

Because in the ten years of marriage Y was continually unhappy and X couldn't take it anymore. Because Y had some shows but they weren't reviewed. Because Y was reviewed but the reviewer wasn't intelligent enough to understand the complexity of what he was doing in his work. Because Y didn't have enough money to make the kind of art he knew he could make if only someone gave Y the chance. Because Y felt like a loser because when filing his income taxes, Y had not made a profit for so many years that his artmaking was deemed a hobby. Because all the art shows Y went to were awful. Because all the artists Y saw in museums and galleries were not as good as Y. Because nobody cares about art anymore, they only care about making money.

So Y, for two weeks at a time, would lie down on the sofa with a pillow over Y's head, only to get up to open another wine bottle. The stench in the house from him not bathing was so bad X left all the windows open, even in the cold of winter, and she would curl up by herself in the guest bedroom with a space heater blasting near her bed, counting the hours and days till the depression would lift. During X's bouts of insomnia she read countless articles on how excessive drinking lowered testosterone levels and affected the quality and quantity of the sperm. Y rarely had a hard-on. And now X had geriatric eggs. The clock ticked. All of X's ancestors were drumming their fingers waiting and waiting for the unborn child.

WITNESSETH THAT:

WHEREAS, it is the desire and intention of the parties, after long and careful consideration, to amicably adjust, compromise, and settle all property rights.

Before a character can make a big decision, they must face a real dilemma. But before that, they have to experience the kind of disaster that leaves them with no good choice.

I make art to not kill myself, Y says. I make art to make love to myself. It's a Pygmalion love, the art loves the art loves the art loves the art. Y can't make art when Y is depressed. Y seems to be always depressed.

X wishes for Y to punch her. To cheat on her. Something she could use against him to walk out. Her mother tells her, isn't it enough that you're not happy?

X finds Y one day in a dark apartment dehydrated from binge drinking. The gas burners are on. The windows are shut. X had been away for the day, not even twenty-four hours. Y did threaten that if X left him alone Y would kill himself. X took the chance. Who says they will kill themselves and actually does it?

X turns off the burners and oven. Y is not dead. The house stinks of the benign mixture of methane and ethane. X learns later that natural gas is not even that lethal. It would take days for anyone to die from it, for the gas to displace the oxygen or for the gas to reach the pilot light and explode. The smell would kill you first. Even this, Y failed at. In the old movies before natural gas, the suicidally inclined would sit on lazy chairs and wait for death to come. The old stove gas was a mix of methane, hydrogen, and carbon monoxide. It didn't take much for it to saturate the blood and starve the brain and nervous system of oxygen. Just a few breaths of it could knock anyone out. A few minutes exposed to it could kill a man. But natural gas?

Suicide hotline:

Operator: How can I help you?
Y: I want to kill myself.
O: How long have you been feeling this way?

Y: Weeks, months, I don't know.

O: Did something happen?

Y: The art world is full of fascists. The museums are funded by fascists. The gallerists go to parties with fascists. Publicly the artists spit on the fascists but in the end they want the fascists to love them.

O: Are you safe? Are you alone?

Y: I am at home. I am not alone. My wife is here beside me. She made me call you. She says she doesn't want me to kill myself. I don't believe her.

Oh, dear Witness, maybe you empathize with X, who is the one filing for the divorce, who has had to put up with ten years of marriage to someone who buried X in so much debt she may never be able to buy herself a house of her own, who for a quarter of her life has felt trapped and alone inside an apartment with Y. Or maybe her choice to stay in such a marriage for so long makes you angry and think, she made her own bed. No one is trapped. She could have left years ago. But this you must know: X was afraid to trigger another bout of rage, another possible suicide attempt, for then how would X live with herself?

Now, you must be wondering what can possibly happen next in this story. We already know that X and Y will get a divorce. But before that decision is made, X will have to work through all the pros and cons. This is the part of the story where a character works through their dilemma before they make their final irrevocable decision.

Reasons to divorce:
- X no longer wants to invest in potential. Even the gallerist understood when to cut Y off. Instead X wants to save for retirement.
- Y no longer believes in his potential. He hates X for making him dependent on her. They were once a team, or so he thought.

- X and Y no longer have sex. Y wants to have sex when he is not depressed. X never wants to have sex with Y. Instead she prefers her vibrator and watching porn of women sitting on each other's faces.
- X has come to believe it will be easier for X to have a baby on her own, because at least then she'll only have one other mouth to feed.
- X is tired of men. Could she ever love a man again? They all stink. They all seem to be predators. They all just want to talk about themselves. She no longer wants to be their servant, their trophy, their whore.
- Y regularly gets anonymous blow jobs and the shame and guilt makes it impossible for him to look X in the eye.
- X and Y rarely eat meals together.
- X and Y no longer sleep in the same bed.
- Y no longer wants to bring a child into this unjust world. X wants a child. This is a nonnegotiable.
- X realizes she married her father.
- Y realizes he married his mother.

Reasons to stay:
- Despite how much X suffers, a part of her finds Y's angry outbursts and verbal abuse pleasurable. Sometimes when Y gets very angry, X pokes at Y so the anger swells, and all his rage feels like a familiar blanket that she can curl up under. She knows all the triggers and shoots them off and watches them blow up around her.
- Y has realized with time that the humiliation and emasculation that come with being with a woman like X, who pays for everything and makes him feel bad about it, is part of his erotic.
- X does not want to disappoint her mother, who says men are no good yet never left her husband, who punched her in the eye, sending her to the hospital, making her miss three days of work, just because she flirted with the butcher in exchange for the best

cut of meat.

- X's parents also don't believe in divorce. Promises are made to be kept.
- X loves their rent-stabilized apartment in a prime location in New York City. They both have rights to it. Y can't afford to move. X is afraid she will have to pay alimony to Y, who has never held a "real" job.
- Y is afraid he will never find someone as generous as X.
- X is afraid she will end up alone forever.

WITNESSETH THAT:

When they married, they made promises to each other. X takes Y and Y takes X to be husband and wife, for better for worse, for richer or poorer, in sickness and in health, to love and cherish, till death do us part. They made a promise at the courthouse. They made a promise in private. I will love you forever. I will never give up on you. We will fight for our love until the end.

X understands that alcoholism is a disease and depression is a mental illness. If she had been afflicted by either, wouldn't she also want to be loved and taken care of unconditionally? Besides, shouldn't artists be given some kind of pass? Can they really make great art without being reckless, being that they are so sensitive to the human condition and the workings of the world?

X wonders if she is being a capitalist asshole because she isn't taking into account that making art is real work. Hard work, in fact. One doesn't have to make money for their work to count, right? She worked as a manager at a restaurant. She found her work fulfilling. She got paid well for it. But is it really Y's fault that some jobs are rewarded monetarily and others are not?

Oh, Witness, you must be wondering, why did X file the divorce papers now and not years ago, when it's clear she has been miserable for a long time? Is it enough to say that every month when she was ovulating, she had hoped that that would be the month she would get pregnant? In truth, despite it all, X really did believe that Y would hit it big, and all their sacrifices would be worth it, and that finally his depression would lift and they would live happily ever after. And, of course, as in any difficult relationship they did have good moments, great moments even, like when he would massage her feet while they laughed over something on TV.

In moments like those, X would think, maybe they should wait it out after all. How many people have weathered the hard moments in their relationships, given each other enough space to get to the other side of it, and fallen back in love? At the very least they may become great life companions. It's possible, right?

But then X gets pregnant.

For years X was no longer interested in having sex with Y, but when Y climbed into her bed, she would pretend to sleep and let him fuck her from behind, her body still, a heavy mass on the mattress. He'd grab her hips and thrust himself inside her, and she imagined the sperm finding its way to her fertile eggs, although geriatric, like the countless videos she watched on YouTube about reproduction.

When she peed on a stick and the plus sign emerged, she understood immediately that she wanted to have the child alone. If she stayed with

Y, she would be trapped inside this marriage forever. He would make it so she would have to take care of him and the baby for another decade, maybe a lifetime, and then it would be too late to ever leave him. They would grow old, holding on to their rent-stabilized apartment, and they would watch everything in it decay, like their bodies. Their child would hate them for being miserable together and ruining his or her possibility of ever having a loving relationship. X knew Y was not going to age well with all the drinking he did, the bags of chips he had for dinner, the cookies he ate for breakfast. He would end up like all the men in her family, limping from missing toes chopped off because they had diabetes. And all that waited for her was a life of sacrifice, having to care for Y in ways that he never could or would care for her.

If she left immediately, he would never have to know this is his child. She would relieve him of the responsibility. She can start over in Miami, where she has some family and some friends, and say the baby is from a hookup at a bar, to a man she didn't even get a name from. People might call her a slut behind her back, they will feel bad for the child who'll never know his or her father, but there is no turning back. She has had the agreement drawn. The lawyer has already cashed their retainer. She will take on all the debt so he'll let her go without a fight. Their only assets: his art, her child.

And for the first time in all her life, if she listens very carefully, she can hear her ancestors clap and clap and clap and clap.

Self-Portrait

KEEP YOUR SKIRT DOWN AND YOUR LEGS CLOSED. WHY DON'T YOU FIX YOUR HAIR? STOP SWITCHING. DON'T BE SMART. DON'T BE FAST. YOU'LL NEVER GET A HUSBAND LIKE THAT. YOU'LL NEVER KEEP A HUSBAND LIKE THAT. I DON'T HAVE A BUNCH OF WOMEN UP AROUND ME. DON'T TELL YOUR GIRLFRIENDS WHAT YOUR MAN DOES IN BED. WHAT CAN YOU EXPECT, HE'S JUST A MAN. YOU GONNA HAVE TO PUT UP WITH SOMETHING. DON'T BE STUPID. DON'T EAT THAT. STAND UP STRAIGHT, YOU ALREADY TALL, NOW YOU WANT TO PUT ON HEELS. SHE DIDN'T HAVE ANY BUSINESS WITH IT ANY WAY. SERVES HER RIGHT. SMILE. STOP GRINNING UP IN PEOPLE'S FACES LIKE YOU'RE SIMPLE. YOU'LL NEVER FIND ANYONE LIKE YOUR DADDY. THE WORLD DON'T CARE ABOUT YOU. YOU GOT TO BE BETTER THAN THEM, THOSE FOLKS ARE NOT YOUR FRIENDS. YOU NEED A GIRDLE. DON'T HAVE A BUNCH OF WOMEN SITTING UP IN YOUR HOUSE. HAVE SOME PEOPLE OVER, MAKE SOME FRIENDS. YOU OUGHT TO JUST QUIT WHILE YOU'RE AHEAD. YOU GOT TO BE ABLE TO TAKE CARE OF A MAN. I BETTER NOT SEE YOU TAKING CARE OF NO MAN. IS THAT WHAT YOU CALL CLEANING? SHUT UP. I HOPE YOU SLEEPING IN A BRA. MAKE SURE YOU DOUCHE REAL GOOD. YOU BETTER FIND YOU A MAN IN COLLEGE. GO TO COLLEGE AND YOU'LL NEVER FIND A MAN. YOU NEED TO JUST FOCUS ON GETTING YOUR LESSON. DON'T LET NOBODY GET OVER ON YOU. THAT'S WHAT YOU GET FOR THINKING. I WOULDN'T DO IT LIKE THAT. YOU ARE SO SELFISH. YOU THINK YOU'RE SO CUTE. NO USE IN CRYING NOW. A HARD HEAD MAKES A SOFT BEHIND. YOU GOT TO RAISE THE GIRLS AND LOVE THE BOYS. DON'T BRING HOME NO NAPPY-HEADED BABIES. YOU SHOULD BE ASHAMED. YOU SHOULD BE ASHAMED. YOU ARE SHAME.

The Patient Records

1.

It begins in the middle like this: the sun sets quietly in a Brooklyn sky. From the top of a hill we can see the Statue of Liberty signaling an idealism long squashed out from our hearts. Even so, trust does not leave the body completely, and I, floating between intent and the unwritten book, am about to hold my hand out to a young man for a prescription drug no doctor will prescribe for me, even though I need it. Instead, they prescribe me medicines I don't want and that don't work.

2.

It's 2017 and I make my way to a section of the borough I have not been to before—somewhere bordering Williamsburg and Bushwick. A nervous kid about eighteen years old meets me in a regular New York deli across from some housing projects. Our agreement is thirty 20 mg pills of Adderall in exchange for $180. I am nervous too. *I need the money first,* he says, holding a prescription bottle tight in his hand. *You don't get the money first,* I say, *I need to see the pills to make sure they are real.* He fidgets. It feels like a setup, so I leave empty-handed. I return to the comfort of my car and experience a familiar sensation, like I can feel the blood in my veins, adrenaline racing, the life of living. Anything can happen. The kid appears at my car window. *Get in the car,* I tell him, *so I can make sure you're not trying to rip me off.* He says he can't get into a stranger's car. He is my height, regular male build for his age, but he probably thinks that I am the police and I am thinking that he is the police. *This isn't going to work*, I say, and speed off.

3.

That feeling that anything can happen at any time is a condition inscribed into my body by the many things that happened to me as kid. Nothing was within my control then and because of this fact I began to understand the randomness of things occurring. A squirrel, for example, can fall from a thin branch the instant you walk under it right onto your face. There's simply no way to plan for things or avoid other things. This is a revolting way of experiencing the world, but I'm also attracted to it. It's a survival strategy. So when the drug dealer sends me a text that says, *That wasn't me. I sent my brother, and my brother can't do anything right*, I rush back in to meet a new guy and a revised scam. The presence of the drug dealer and my acting beyond the boundaries of reason surely signal, to the reader, an addiction; I understand this. I don't know how to make a compelling case for some other relationship to the drugs I'm trying and failing to obtain.

4.

A certain difficulty lies in the difference between what we want and what we need. Conventional wisdom would have it that in order to differentiate between desire and requirement one must first be able access the past using memory. You have to figure out when memory is about a real happening, a pure feeling, or comes from made-up thoughts. For Freud, memory determines much of who we are (the beingness of being). When one has access to recalled memory, it presents, first, I think, in images and then the brain kicks in to do its interpretation work. We like to think about our memories. We like to ask questions about what occurred, about what we don't remember or what was outside of the frame entirely. Want can only come from the mind, if you buy into this theory, and what we know about ourselves and believe ourselves to remember, while need is more precise, I think, but also more suspect. The body can have its own needs including, but not limited to, the nutrients that one must have for survival. But, when another person says, *I need you*, we think they are really referring to desire.

5.

I have a memory, akin to one you have, maybe, from a photograph in my mother's photo album. I'm about three years old, dressed for church—it might be Easter—in a light blue dress and cape, and holding an open yellow umbrella above my head. It appears to me that I look forlorn and I remember keenly a forlorn feeling, trapped in the outfit and white tights and black patent-leather Mary Janes. My mother loved Mary Janes in her own youth and nostalgically purchased them for me, attempting, it seems, to hold on to time. She loves old-fashioned candy like Squirrel Nut Zippers and records on vinyl and Charlie Pride, born one year after her, and the Grand Ole Opry on the radio. I do not remember wearing the dress, but I do remember the house I'm standing in front of in the photo. It was in a part of town that my parents wanted to get away from, and did eventually, touching down in a part of town more integrated, which meant better.

6.

I no longer remember being inside of the child body dressed in soft blue, but I can still feel its precarious existence, and its knowing, even so, a possible power that might be accessed. One day, when I was older, four or five, I was playing outside on the old metal railing in front of the house's side door. When I fell from the railing, I did so in a way where I landed on my child vagina, my legs splayed on either side of the bar. I had done this to myself but now it would have to be investigated, which meant exposure of a part of my body I hadn't yet thought about in any significant way. In moments like these, one becomes the body's flesh, skeletal scaffold, and blood. I imagine this child-body laid out on a silver examining table, under a stark gaze, yet somehow invisible. My mother wanted to check to see if I was bleeding given that the fall had caused me to wail hysterically, inconsolably. I don't remember if I was taken to the doctor or what happened after. I remember nothing else except a shadow feeling of being in the kind of pain that happens to bones.

7.

Time is not linear; instead it's like a strong breath tunneling up through experience and spreading out, inhabiting a body. A body can be infinite as much as it's a mechanism for processing food. When my mother tells me a story, it's as if time has stood still for her. No partition between the past and the future. No influence of one upon the other. She glances around her present surroundings, a vacant look in her eyes, and tells me about the time her uncle pulled a gun on some white men asking for directions. *They weren't asking for directions*, she says with a tilt of the head. It was night. A gas station somewhere way out in swamplands. I can picture those white men and the goofy frivolity of their violence and my mother's uncle and whoever else was in the car like apparitions in the room. One person's good-old-boy fun is another person's dismemberment, is their dogged haunting. I, too, am trying to concentrate on something outside of time.

8.

I tell you all of this—the fall from the railing, the nonmemory of wearing the blue dress, the man with his hand shaking, likely, around a rifle pointed at some white guys' heads—as a way of blurring the distinction between desire and need and highlighting the possibility for nonlinear time. Also, I want you to know me better. Those memories and not-memories are also ways for me to three-dimensionalize the depths of my person as a character in this narrative. But here's some advice: don't try to talk to a medical professional about nonlinear time. The professions are there to tell you what you need and to disparage what you know to be true. I am very uncertain about the function of memories of the past and how they work if time is not a thing that we are simply marching through, or that's marching through us. It can be challenging to develop your own idea of things when regulated by professionals' bright laboratories. Those professionals with their badges of knowledge will look directly at the burning sore on your asshole and tell you that it cannot be from the medication they prescribed you. It's a fungus, they tell you, cause unknown, produced by the body of its own accord. The badge-wearers tell you to take another medicine to cure the fungus, but they don't tell you that the other medicine can make you sterile. Or, you enter the emergency medical center with a sore throat, and the doctors—two of them—say it's probably gonorrhea and that you should probably get antibiotic injections right now before the test results come back. Your mouth falls open. You are 99 percent sure that you do not have gonorrhea of the throat but for a minute you actually consider the injections.

9.

All the ways your body is a site for investigation, someone else's false documentary. Many years ago, when I was a graduate student, I accepted my psychiatrist's invitation to participate in an ADHD study. The psychiatrist and I had the relationship that most patients have with their mental health doctors. I was under his care. In his care I could help him understand things about medicines for the mind. Or, at the very least, the way these medicines worked or did not work on me. It seemed like he was trying to find the perfect balance of medications to help me. He did this by changing my medicines and dosages periodically in a similar way that I might, not being a doctor. When I entered the ADHD study, I was hungover most of the time. No one asked me if I was hungover, and I wonder now if this influenced the result of the study. The psychologist who administered the tests—twenty hours of them—was very kind but had distractingly small hands and feet, like a child's. Rather conclusively, the psychologist with the tiny extremities determined that I did not have ADHD. She became my therapist after that, and I would sit in her office once a week, telling her some things but not others, mostly looking at the child-sized rain boots on the corner mat. I didn't tell her about the vaginal wound. I thought she might read too much into it. Or the wrong things. She liked to view most things through the lens of conflict. She would say, If there's not a conflict there's not a problem. My primary problems were a deep sadness, anxiety, and also that I was having a lot of anonymous sexual encounters. I call them "encounters" because they weren't sex exactly. And the people didn't feel like people. It was mostly jerking off and inappropriate touching, sometimes with force: all sex games with pre-articulated rules. We met in secret, barely trafficked places. The encounters struck me as dangerous and the danger rose in my blood, propelling me toward the faceless, nameless bodies. The conflict was that I was doing something potentially harmful but I was unsure whether I wanted to be harmed.

10.

The anonymous sexual encounters were situated somewhere between need and want. They were also a way toward a reckoning, peeling back the skin to see what's underneath, what you're really made of. No one told me to do it. The actions just occurred to my body. I began to avoid all the other activities in my life, which became tatters around the edges, whispering my name. The encounters are how I know what I know about time, how it can shrink down inside itself and become like a black hole in outer space even as a day, for instance, turns from light to dark. I learned another thing, more practical, about how the creatures you meet in the dark are not all monsters. Or maybe the converse was my true education—that monsters often inhabit the light, look just like rest of us, have regular jobs. Their monstrous acts appear small and relatively harmless.

11.

Once a month I went to the psychiatrist, the one with the prescriptions. He didn't ask me about conflict or how I spent my days. He asked me how I was feeling. I couldn't focus on anything. The depressed state was alleviated but persisted. I thought I wanted to live. The stars of this imaginary documentary, the one about my body but not me, are two doctors whose offices are located in different buildings. They peer into the same test-tube body yet never speak to each other, secure in their individual conclusions. If I had known that a body can become a kind of object as it seeks relief, I would have told them both what they needed to know so that they could write a joint paper. It would recommend listening outside of what they think they know about the mind and memory and the uncertain balance of anyone's psyche. I knew, for example, that the conclusion from the ADHD tests was incorrect. I didn't know how to tell them that the fire that occupied me when my body was in potential danger was evidence to this fact. In other words, when my heart raced, when adrenaline pulsed through my veins, focus and calm kicked in, a feeling of equilibrium. I do not mean this to be evidence, but discovery. An internal landscape, partially mapped.

12.

My mother provides evidence in the false documentary. Standing outside of time, she is young and thin again, on a beach boardwalk with her sister, wearing a one-piece bathing suit and sunhat, smiling. What she does not know in this moment is that she will marry a man who will move her thousands of miles away from her family and that this man will not love her, nor she him. She tells the doctors, *I have a girl child in your future. The girl child is an intellectual. She reads and reads.* My mother does not know about the fire like a hot poker pressing inside my belly. The knowledge evades her in any configuration of time. I am beyond her world partitioned by the contours of a small body in view and the believed wholesomeness of a girl's existence: this, whatever I am.

13.

I know better now than to ask any doctor for what I need, lest it be confused with want. There is nothing left for memory in service of medicine. If you give them your memories, they'll likely see the prefigured drawings carved into their textbooks. What is held in the secret, mysterious spaces of our bodies? Throughout my entire childhood, I got nosebleeds of the epic sort. They came on suddenly, blood pouring out of my nose like a warning, until a washcloth filled with ice placed on the bridge of my nose slowed the bleeding and big clots formed that I'd snort out. There are some radical researchers who write about what the body holds, and what that holding does to the body and the mind. They tell us that the body holds trauma and doesn't even know it because that holding produces an extreme disconnect from the body. And, even so, the body has to deal with that stress situation of trauma, and we can't know what that will be like inside each person. Still, not everything is known.

14.

The ways toward transformation are mysterious. That a partial healing of the psyche occurred in whatever tangential way it happened, outside of medical prescriptions and the doctors' claims about care, surprised me. It was intuition that drove me to allow strangers the sexual use of my body, even though I sometimes called that intuition "compulsion." And it was this compulsion that enabled a purging. Something had been stuck inside my body, and I needed to work it out. The need for danger may have been a desire for death. The overindulgence in the courting of death moved through me because it had nowhere else to go. Free from it, I could focus on my actual sexual desires, not the driving obligations that felt like service instruments, but the ones that lived deep inside my being. The instruments allowed me to eject a good deal of vaginal hurt. Vaginal hurt, in this case, is a vast landscape of pain that includes what has been inflicted on the gendered body (female) and the vulnerable availability of the child body. I was still in therapy at the time and visiting the psychiatrist for pills. Once I could feel myself on the other side of my obscene and secret process, I fired them both and stopped taking all the medicines.

15.

Years go by. All around me, change. I watch the boy next door grow into a young man. I accomplish some things. Post-medication, I have to relearn how to feel the range of what's to be felt. Anxiety and depression occasionally still send me into days of waste. The first time I take an ADHD drug it's recreationally. A friend gives me Adderall to take in any way I want. I don't yet know their power, and I take one at a conference in Boston during a blizzard. Imagine the knee-deep snow and more falling heavy like stones, blinding wind, the conference-goers stumbling around and falling in the middle of streets, everyone underdressed in a weird state of disbelief. But for me, it's the first time in years when I haven't had to binge on alcohol in order to negotiate an intense social situation. Suddenly, the excitement of it all does not overwhelm. I feel okay. Like, I feel fine in an even way. I'm in place, which is to say, the snow is beautiful.

16.

I found my way onto the dark web after Dr. R, a psychiatrist who only does video conferencing, convinced me that I should try Cymbalta. This was after I had clearly communicated to her that I did not want to take long-term antidepressants because it had taken me years to wean myself off them when I fired my doctors back in graduate school. I told her this before the video meeting and again at the meeting itself, which was before she charged my credit card $400, if you're still interested in conventional notions of time. Stupidly, I had also told her that my preferred medicine was for ADHD, that I found it calming. I had expressed my needs. I had drawn a line in the sand. This is what we've been told to do as women, to be empowered agents of our own destinies, yes?

17.

Ignoring this request, she did a good talking up of Cymbalta's possibilities. She seemed like she'd long been practicing the contortion of the face to appear empathetic. Same goes for her intonation. I was having a hard time seeing things as they were, and her performance created a tiny bubble of hope in the center of my throat. A bubble that popped almost immediately, because one introductory dose of Cymbalta turned me into a zombie. My arms and legs buzzed, but at the same time I couldn't feel them. A pall was pulled down over the space between me and everything outside my body. I could scream, *There's someone alive in here!*, but no one would hear me. Dr. R, via a texting mechanism associated with the video-conferencing mechanism, said that I could be "a little tired" for up to two weeks but then I'd feel better. This was a lie. People on message boards talked about debilitating fatigue lasting months. They were stuck in the space between living and dying, with only those like them—or those afraid of becoming them—to listen to their claims of discomfort. I had a book to finish. Dr. R knew this, but she didn't seemed to understand that there's a symbiotic relationship between the creative mind at work and the transformation of psychic pain. The rest of the pills are tucked in the recesses of my medicine cabinet, if you want them. I told Dr. R that I had to find a psychiatrist with more imagination—one who did not insist, for instance, that there was no evidence that microdosing LSD or hallucinogenic mushrooms can have an effect on existential ailments that dig out the psyche. There is something beyond Freud and Lacan and Jung, my mother, the ego, the pathology of desire, and anchor events. I wanted to believe Dr. R, but she wanted to schedule another $400 meeting.

18.

One Virtual Private Network (VPN), one Bitcoin account, and one TOR search engine later, and I'm on the dark web where, admittedly, some of the most horrible beings on God's green earth lurk and organize and build connections toward some unimaginable catastrophe. But the mechanism itself is not monstrous, however much it allows for the worst of humanity to indulge in brutality. The dark expansive wildernesses of Mississippi are not responsible for the bloodshed, lynchings, and cutting of genitalia. It's a mutated kind of person who makes the sacred land a wet burial ground for murdered lambs. And what to do when you must enter the wild forests at night anyway? They provide your cloak too, as scary and risky as it all is.

19.

In your future, a small package will arrive stuffed into the mailbox. No return address. The package contains four small capsules hidden in the lining of a disposable garment. They are individually packaged by the manufacturer. No matter the signs that seem to point toward the drug's legitimacy, you have a panic attack immediately after your test run when you open one of the capsules and pour some of the contents into your mouth. You begin sweating and you feel like you're going to pass out. *It's poison*, a voice from nowhere says. *Oh my God, I'm dying*, another voice in your head screams. The voices quiet when death doesn't come stabbing. About 45 minutes later, you're sitting on your patio writing this very essay and feeling quite at ease.

20.

A friend once told me that her mother is the quintessentially Indian mother, meaning that her mother's goal is to anticipate and fulfill her children's needs before they even know they have them. That seems impossible, I told my friend. What if she anticipates incorrectly? To me it sounded like a fictional creation of the child's reality, a planting of foreign seeds into a consciousness as a means toward control. I told my friend this, too, insensitive to any cultural notions beyond my experience. I went even further: It seems very colonialist, I said. I think of the girl in the photo at Easter. All the props that construct that image. A camera's lens often shirks its responsibility of transparency. In this case, however, the image profoundly reveals the erasure of the girl. Someone had asked that I place one hand on my hip, because there the hand is on the hip; the other hand holds the yellow umbrella, though it is not raining. But I have never willingly placed my hand on my hip for a photo.

21.

Rebellion happens in my eyes, which refuse to look up at the camera; my head is cast slightly downward, as if to say simply, *No*. If I am creating my own story, and I guess I am, the sunken forests, darknets, and shaded eyes are not where I gather my strength for resistance. It is here, in the light, with all of you, on the airy side of the blinded window alongside the micromonsters and everything else.

22.

In the documentary I make of myself, I am lying on a beach where time is slowed and stretched out, making the body soft like blue light. My mother tells me for the hundredth time that she told her primary-care physician for the hundredth time that the injections they gave her have made her crippled. She's stuck inside this conversation that begins, I know what caused my pain, and ends with the doctor saying, *There is no reason for your pain*. I am reminded of Joan Didion's reporting in *The White Album* about Huey Newton being shot in the stomach, and the trial of Newton that follows. In the transcript of the trial, a nurse tells of his refusal to prove his insurance coverage and sign documents as he is bleeding from the gunshot wound. The nurse claims that even though he has been shot in that sensitive organ, he's not in any "acute distress." The presence of the human body and its language do not provide good evidence, apparently, about the experience of the person, depending on who that person is.

23.

My mother and I time-travel, in my documentary, to a far-flung coast on the Mediterranean Sea to talk to each other. In this way, we escape time and its trappings. We escape the world that claims to know us better than we know ourselves. I tell her that once I tried to buy ADHD drugs from a fake drug dealer in Bed Stuy who cheated me and gave me allergy meds instead. Nobody was listening to me, I tell her, so I had to listen to the sound of my own heart. What do I want from her, my mother, outside of time and the labor of her sagging living room where, in the other world, she always is? We doze a little in our chaise longues, the ocean rhythms like the beat of existence. When we wake, she says, *There are so many ways that they don't see us, just as I've never seen you.*

BLACK OXIMETER

Outside city hall, black folks stand in a long queue that circles around the city. One endlessly long line. There were ten different makeshift medical office kiosks. The black folks arrive from all over the country to find out if they are alive or dead. They wait in line for only one reason: 1) at each kiosk, they hold out their wrists for the white people to hear, read, measure their pulse.

BLACK MAN: What did you hear?

WHITE MAN: A pulse.

BLACK MAN: Am I still alive?

WHITE MAN: Yes

BLACK MAN: Are you sure?

WHITE MAN: I think so.

BLACK MAN: You think so or you know so?

WHITE MAN: You have a pulse.

BLACK MAN: And you think it means I am still alive.

WHITE MAN: Medically speaking.

BLACK MAN: Racially speaking?

WHITE MAN: Racially speaking, I think you are not dead.

BLACK MAN: Do you want me to die?

WHITE MAN: No

BLACK MAN: Then, how could you feel my pulse?

WHITE MAN: I wear a lab coat.

BLACK MAN: I thought you were a cop.

WHITE MAN: What's that?

BLACK MAN: You tell me.

WHITE MAN: The dictionary says "a conical or cylindrical roll of thread wound onto a spindle"

BLACK MAN: There are so many definitions for it, why did you choose that one?

WHITE MAN: It makes me less accountable, I think.

BLACK MAN: Are you Asian?

WHITE MAN: No.

BLACK MAN: Do you wear a conical hat?

WHITE MAN: No.

BLACK MAN: Then how do you know that I am not dead?

WHITE MAN: I checked your pulse.

BLACK MAN: With what?

WHITE MAN: With—

BLACK MAN: Your gun?

WHITE MAN: My fingers, my index and middle.

BLACK MAN: What happened to your thumb?

WHITE MAN: It's hard to do an accurate reading with my thumb.

BLACK MAN: Do you think I am dumb?

WHITE MAN: No.

BLACK MAN: hen why did you not use your thumb?

WHITE MAN: I am a doctor.

BLACK MAN: Sure you are.

WHITE MAN: can guarantee that you have a pulse.

BLACK MAN: You can guarantee that I will have a pulse.

WHITE MAN: You have one already.

BLACK MAN: You used the tip of my own gun to measure my own pulse?

WHITE MAN: I could use a pulse oximeter if you want me to.
BLACK MAN: Am I dead?
WHITE MAN: No.
BLACK MAN: Am I dead?
WHITE MAN: No.
BLACK MAN: Am I dead?
WHITE MAN: No.
BLACK MAN: Am I dead?
WHITE MAN: No.
BLACK MAN: Am I dead?
WHITE MAN: No.
BLACK MAN: Am I dead?
WHITE MAN: No.
BLACK MAN: Am I dead?
WHITE MAN: No.
BLACK MAN: Am I dead?
WHITE MAN: No.
BLACK MAN: Am I dead?
WHITE MAN: No.
BLACK MAN: Am I dead?
WHITE MAN: No.
BLACK MAN: Am I dead?
WHITE MAN: No.
BLACK MAN: Am I dead?
WHITE MAN: Yes.
BLACK MAN: Good boy.
WHITE MAN: Thank you.
BLACK MAN: We finally agree on something.
WHITE MAN: I'm scared.
BLACK MAN: Why?
WHITE MAN: It's harder to kill a dead person.

BLACK MAN: It is, isn't it?
WHITE MAN: Sure is.

Notes on Writing about Sexual Violence

"What would happen," the poet Muriel Rukeyser asks in her oft-quoted poem "Käthe Kollwitz," "if one woman told the truth about / her life? / The world would split open." Over the past few years, I've begun to question that quote, especially as it relates to telling the truth about sexual violence. What is the purpose and function of writing about rape? More to the point, what is the purpose and function of writing *for me* when writing about my rape? These questions grew more painful to consider after I published my first book examining the long-term effects of violence and survival, and more painful still when I learned this book had apparently ended up on the reading lists of various tastemakers on Twitter, one of whom informed that she was using the book as a writing prompt for her own students' exploration of violence. Thus my private experience was to become a "jumping-off point" for others' creativity, my descriptions of my assault apparently disseminated and refracted through the formal exercises of strangers in order to understand the effects of such violence themselves, so that my assault would become both symbol and trope, something that could be parsed and imitated until all the rage and humanness drained out of it. This was, of course, one of the possible outcomes of publishing such a book, one that ended up in the maw of social media.

Speak truth to power, writers and nonwriters alike declaim, and now this phrase has become the battle cry of Facebook and Twitter:

to tell the truth of our lives as we see it, as directly and with as little remorse as possible. Such an outpouring of personal testimony has indeed cracked open the world, in part by reminding participants in social media that what most American institutions want happily to forget about our nation stubbornly persists—its violence against people of color, its killing of LGBTQ people, its seemingly implacable hatred of women and their bodies that permeates political and religious institutions alike. There is indeed a power and value to truth-telling, but most of us forget that truth-telling relies upon narrative, and that narrative telling—even supposedly artless, immediate telling—is in fact crafted for particular responses, and nothing crafts language so effectively as a Web format that requires you to express yourself in 280 characters or less, and which sells these truth-telling nuggets in a stream of visual media that makes it impossible to focus on anything but the most extreme, most compelling, and most direct language.

Social media and truth-telling both encourage the reader, primarily, to emote. And having emoted, having felt all of the things and thought all of the thoughts the writer has asked us to think and feel within such a limited format, we can thus walk away from the engagement satisfied with the blunt, brute fact of our feelings. Or perhaps, as I saw from the young woman's response to my book, we might replicate these feelings in writing we produce ourselves in order to garner some of that same attention, that same veneer of authenticity that claims the authority of survivorship and thus makes autobiography and resilience satisfactory political goals.

A book about a sexual assault from a first-person position guarantees a certain amount of attention, because it is sensational and because writing about violence encourages a kind of voyeurism on the part of the reader, who's implicitly being asked to imagine herself as a victim of events she may or may not ever have suffered herself. But while this may be one possible response, it is not the writer's desire to make the reader participate in the imagined construction of violence by rewriting its events. And it is not what we teach other budding writers about the purpose of testimonies about violence, in particular the testimonies about violence that women might produce. If anything, we argue, women's testimonies of violence should inspire not empathy (or not only empathy) but political outrage, in large part because women's autobiographical writing has been so effectively suppressed over centuries. Women's writing about violence serves still as a public novelty, one which, if it does not always receive the socially approved status of high literary art, at least promises its readers to be an authentic expression of rage, of grief, of endurance and survival, and—most powerfully—of hope.

But I'm not actually that interested in resilience. I want jail time for offenders. I want politicians tossed out of office, priests defrocked, federal judges fired and replaced. I want a country that doesn't treat violence against women as sexual entertainment. I want to watch my assaulter burn.

Over the past year, I've begun to hate this book I've published, largely because the more I read from and about it, the more politically and aesthetically suspicious my own writing appears to me. Who had I written it for? Who did I really imagine as its audience? The book started, in part, as a reaction to the 2009 Lilly Ledbetter Fair Pay Act, which got me thinking about the ways in which sex discrimination has shaped my working life, which got me thinking about the sexual assault I experienced as a twenty-year-old woman at a coat factory where I worked one summer as a down stuffer along with several itinerant workers, one of whom attacked me. The book was finally published around the time our current president, then a presidential candidate, admitted to grabbing women "by the pussy," which made the Me Too hashtag started by Tarana Burke in 2006 erupt into a firestorm promulgated primarily on social media. Into this storm my own book was tossed, and while I was happy at first to add my voice to the movement, over time I began to feel that the book sounded less like my individual voice than an automated reply. If the language the rapist and the abuser uses to describe women feels crude and rote, so too does the language the media uses to depict sexual abuse; if my attacker saw me as little more than my sexual parts, I have also been reduced to a crude sexual term by a young female writer ostensibly sympathetic to my experience, who related, in an email to me, how shocked she was to picture a man "forcing himself inside [my] pussy." As a writer, I am more than a little dismayed to find myself—or anyone—relying upon or creatively navigating the same tropes and images and events that a thousand other women *and* their abusers use to construct the violence that has (if temporarily) disempowered women. To use the same language that has characterized the experience of so many other women certainly brings me into community with them, but it also makes the stories I read from other survivors feel depressingly interchangeable and flat.

Perhaps this flattening out of our individual stories is created in part by our social expectation of what comprises female psychology and women's writing, in particular our assumption that women's writing is primarily or only autobiographical, not imaginative, and that it stems from an institutionally disadvantaged position that we equate fundamentally with pain. This, too, enrages me. Apparently, because I am female, I was born into this language and psychology; I was prepared to tell the story of my assault since I was twelve years old and heard one of my best friends tell me about being raped by her drunk father. Since I was fourteen and followed home in a car by a man who hissed filthy racial slurs at me. Since learning from another friend in college that the best way to protect yourself from one angry man is to offer to sleep with another, possibly less angry one. These, apparently, were the stories available to me and that, like it or not, shaped me. According to all these stories, as a woman and a writer, I am a grievance waiting to be heard and endured, and at times it feels that the best I can do is pay close attention to that grievance, to give it a slightly different shape and coloration. By writing about my grief, my anger, my assault, I am now able to inhabit fully my femininity. By writing about my assault, I thus confirm what is the most inarguably authentic position of the not-male, and also the not-white: the pained, the wounded, the helpless, the *small*.

To speak about one's assault in any way that feels actually authentic is to thread the needle through an incredibly slender eye made ever more narrow by the pressure of therapeutic services, which argue that such narratives are not only good but necessary for psychic healing, and by political and social institutions, which argue that truth-telling makes for good rallying cries and possible legislation, and narrowed further still by social media, which argues for ever more devastating expressions of the self to be streamed and consumed and disseminated.

Writing effectively about violence shares many of the same aesthetic traits with political language, as well as writing on social media, which is to say that its directness resists excessive or subtle interpretation. It compresses time and context in order to focus on the moment at hand. Writing about violence authenticates itself through the performance of immediacy and vivid feeling. This is what constitutes truth, and it is surprisingly, distressingly easy to duplicate.

All of which is to say that *this* is why the social media performances of grief, selfhood, and outrage we daily read feel like suspiciously like masquerades. In our feeds, we try to outshine and outthink the politicians and abusers inspiring our outrage, using language whose syntax and complexity rarely rise above their own, meaning we are shackled to our shadow doubles, meaning that as much as I despise the self-help books, the prayer circles, the thin whine of grief on Twitter and its overuse (and continual *mis*use) of the word *trauma*, I understand that the only identity that cannot be challenged or shamed is that of the victim, and so I see myself and others willingly write into and about how we have been diminished or shamed so as to stop ourselves from being attacked by strangers online, because apparently the only thing to keep oneself safe online is to become the witting accomplice in your own self-objectification.

Added to that is the problem that refracting and repeating narratives of violence risk also downplaying or even ignoring specifics of race and class in favor of the sensational act of the violence itself, even as race and class make some part of this violence more or less likely for certain people to experience. It is not lost on me, for example, that I came from a middle-class family but was attacked by someone skirting the poverty line, and that what brought us together was the coat factory that relied on both our labor to exist: me, the mixed-race college student earning money for her next year's tuition; my attacker, a white man who moved from job to job, city to city, aimless and resentful, apparently, of the future and opportunities I had in a world that he imagined pandered to minorities. It is not lost on me either that the stories we repeat most often are those narrated by and about white women, and that our retweeting and sharing of these stories in some sense replicates the culture's co-opting of Tarana Burke's Me Too hashtag into the world of (largely) white and (largely) middle-class feminism.

All of which is exactly what this young woman, consciously or unconsciously, performed when she imitated my own writing. She understood that some part of writing about and against violence, especially the violence that women experience, is imitative and coercive. You do not have to be the victim of violence to render that violence believably or powerfully. The actual experience of an assault may be private, it may reveal the world to be artless and cruel, but the sharing of it depends entirely upon creative skills and images and ideas of identities that can be appropriated.

***

When I first thought to write my book, I assumed that writing about my assault might lead to some personal catharsis. I'd also fantasized it might do what Rukeyser suggested: split open the world. Obviously, my writing has not accomplished either of these goals. It has not made me a healthier person, it has not erased or even much eased the memory of my assault, and, while it may have helped shine a brighter light on a truth we have long known exists, it has certainly not helped change the very nature of that truth: to bring the responsible parties to justice, to hold institutions of power accountable. In that, my book's failure is hardly unique. Month after month after month, the Me Too stories pile up. Another book or essay or blog post is published, the poem goes viral, people read and share on social media and weep and publish think pieces and gather writers on radio and talk shows, and what happens? The pussy-grabber is elected president, a man accused of trying to rape a fellow high school student gets a permanent seat on the Supreme Court. A wave of anti-choice and anti-women laws rolls across the southern states with little prospect of being stopped. Church after church admits to sex abuse scandals, and yet somehow the priests are moved to other parishes while the highest-up administrators remain in place. For months it seems the only person who appears to suffer any consequences for his behavior is a movie mogul who everyone knew was scum, and whose movies hardly anyone watches anymore.

Of course, I never *really* believed my writing would change the world. I know such a thing takes more concrete and practical steps: the daily, basic work of trying to keep your democracy from going up in flames. So, like millions of other women, I write the letters and go to the marches and stump for the politicians and work at the conventions and sacrifice money and time on the altar of American politics because

I believe such activism is the herd immunity against fascism we are each responsible for maintaining, even if we are at times unsure of our general affiliation with the herd; even if we suspect that our current politicians would really just prefer the vast majority of us fall sick and die.

Still, I wonder what role writing, and writing about sexual violence, is meant to play in the social sphere. Added to that, what *kind* of language is most effective for achieving these imagined goals? Is it literary language, which as a writer I've been taught to revere and emulate, or is it the easily disposable and increasingly formulaic language of our feeds, which even as I personally decry it, I can't help but recognize has forced us all to the table? If it hasn't gotten all the offending politicians tossed out, it's certainly ended or at least stunted certain careers. It's altered HR policies and made us look newly askance at power dynamics in class, and it's even got some in religious institutions arguing whether women should be able to preach. It's reshaped the language we use around race and violence and gender in our interpersonal interactions, if not in our courts and in our administrations. In that, social media has provided us with a far more effective tool than anything my own professors and fellow activists had at hand in the 1990s, during the first wave of what critics dismissed as the "political correctness" movement. But even as I write this, I recognize that the classroom and the dinner party and the campus quad and the NPR roundtable are hardly enough. I want a different nation. In that case, what is the language that will achieve that?

Perhaps my hatred of my book is just internalized misogyny, but I prefer to see it as an ethical problem: What is the language that insists upon and reifies both our group identity and our individuation? Is there a language like that which exists for women? Do we have to be seen as people not produced first by pain in order to write effectively about it, to have that expression of pain become socially galvanizing?

And, even as I write this, it also strikes me that perhaps I'm wrong to think we've become numb or jaded about female narratives of pain. I think back to that look on Arizona senator Jeff Flake's face in the elevator as he fled the Kavanaugh hearings, the moment when a protestor pried apart the elevator doors to demand he listen to the assault that she'd survived. I see again the obvious pain twist across his face. Perhaps the reason the Me Too movement hasn't succeeded in achieving more substantial victories for women is not because its language has started to feel formulaic, but because it really *is* too painful for people to witness. It's too painful because it asks those who have not suffered to imagine the limits of their own physical invulnerability—to realize, if only empathetically, that their sense of self-protection is a fantasy. We turn away from the language of violence not because it has become anodyne, but because we see how easily each of us can be made a victim.

***

Here's something from my life, and about my understanding about my assault, that I did not include in my book.

Many years ago, I lived with a man who'd been raped as a child. This man wasn't a writer, never wanted to construct a narrative about his experience, never even wanted to speak to me about it. It was only the slow, painful death of our relationship that compelled him, finally, to admit what he'd suffered. Even then, my boyfriend didn't tell me much about what happened, but he told me enough. My boyfriend, like many children, knew his rapist. This rapist was a mentally disturbed cousin who lived with my boyfriend's grandparents in a run-down cabin my boyfriend and his brother visited each summer. The cabin had only an outhouse for a bathroom, my boyfriend told me, so the cousin would watch and wait for my boyfriend—then twelve years old—to go to the outhouse, at which point he'd follow him in.

You might think that a man who'd been raped would make a perfect romantic partner for a woman who'd also been sexually assaulted, but it turns out to be the exact opposite. While he was kind to me, tender, would never have dreamed of hurting me, my boyfriend was also skittish and paranoid. While I only learned of his rape a month or two before we broke up, in retrospect I see that his assault affected every aspect of our two-year relationship. My boyfriend was highly suspicious of women, particularly of women who he said "claimed" to be raped. He saw them as manipulative, he said, victims who lacked the mental fortitude to protect themselves. For this reason, we often argued about feminism and politics, about women's sexual agency, about what it meant when a woman said "no." For this reason, I never told him I'd been attacked. I knew it would only confirm his worst suspicions, that it would inspire disgust and fear in him, not sympathy.

Of course, when my boyfriend finally admitted his own rape to me, some part of his paranoia and misogyny made sense. It wasn't mistrust of women but envy I think that motivated my boyfriend's anger, the sense that he'd been abandoned by family and society, left to his own devices to deal with the aftermath. My boyfriend refused to see a therapist. At the time he was coming to terms with his childhood abuse, he knew (or suspected) that there were no support groups, no therapeutic movements around male rape survivors. Even the word rape itself conjured (and perhaps still conjures) solely male perpetrators and solely female victims. My boyfriend was also a large man, six foot five and 250 pounds. No one would have imagined, or believed, he could be a victim of assault. Added to all of this was the newly in-vogue '90s term *sexual harassment*, which for my twenty-three-year-old boyfriend—himself still trying to discern the rules for appropriate and inappropriate male desire—meant that women could, at any time, accuse a man of unwanted attention and be believed. Believed in ways my boyfriend felt that he, as a child and as a man, would never have been.

My boyfriend was trying to survive in a society that had made him the victim of sexual abuse but refused to imagine he could also be one, that offered him no therapeutic language or spaces, that offered him no communal identity that didn't also suggest he must reframe his sexual orientation from straight to gay. In other words, there was no culturally understood identity for my boyfriend to perform and be healed by.

When I bemoan the ways in which female identity gets elided with victimhood, and the way social media has only made this imagined relationship more performative, let me also say that I see some benefit to that in a culture where women are statistically highly likely to be attacked, molested, and raped. Having no language, I believe, is worse than having too much of it, and if I fear at times that I've disappeared into the dark narrative of female life shadowing me since birth, I can also appreciate the terror of stepping blind into the glare of a spotlight that shines on you alone. Even at age twenty-three, I understood there was no language around rape that wouldn't have rendered my boyfriend more vulnerable, more terribly seen. Then, and possibly now, my boyfriend's confession would be socially galvanizing, far more so than my own, but it also might be personally ruinous.

At the same time, my boyfriend's automatic rejection of the term *victim*, his knee-jerk misogyny also told me just how much women's testimony and female identity remain social anathema. My boyfriend didn't just hate being seen as a rape victim, he hated what being a rape victim implied, which was that he was now just like a woman.

Again, it's probably not just likely but inevitable that I've internalized this same misogyny. Perhaps my struggle to find a language adequate to express my own assault is less about my frustrated political desires and my dislike of social media and far more about my fear that I write like a woman; that so long as I am compelled to write about what happens to me and those like me, the tastemakers and critics and "high art" consumers and prize committees won't take me seriously; I'll never be judged as having produced a book that gives me the same credibility and authority as a man.

Overall, however, I think my anger is due to the fact that, whether the language renders us invisible or hypervisible, "female" or "male," believable or not believable, however we express the violence we've experienced, that language is not finally controlled, owned, or authored only by us. Our language is taken from us by the audience that consumes it, by the media that reports on it, by the technology that perpetuates and capitalizes upon it. As much as our writing about sexual violence purports to slip outside the systems of institutional control we want to critique, it can't. The language becomes owned or policed by sites like Facebook, co-opted by politicians and social movements that have little real investment in our own psychic rehabilitation. It is repeated and consumed, shared, spread, and rendered unremarkable. In a corporate culture in which anything can be purchased, social media has taken away the real power of personal testimony and replaced it with the *image* of power, the suggestion that immediate self-expression is tantamount to individuation, even as the algorithms suppress actual individuation in favor of interchangeable mob approval. If the last election proved that outside forces can use social media to disrupt elections, it also proved that Twitter and Facebook and Instagram work as perfect social controls for those eager to work inside a capitalist system that purports to reward the active self-promoter: we can sell more of ourselves to ourselves. In that, our attempts to change via these systems negate any actual change.

Some part of my boyfriend understood that, I think: not about the role social media plays in testimony, as social media hadn't yet been invented, but about the nature of privacy, the limits of confession in a culture hungry to absorb people's personal information. He understood those limits for exactly the wrong, and terrible, reasons, but his reluctance to confess what had happened to him was, I think, also based on the knowledge that he could not forever control or return to that language once he said it aloud. Once he spoke about what had happened to him, it would become a story—one he was no longer the sole author of, as I'm proving to you now.

My ex died recently, and I don't know if he told other people what happened to him. I assume he told his wife, perhaps having seen how his silence negatively affected our relationship, which was as loving and supportive as it could have been at a time when both of us believed—but never admitted to each other—that we thought our lives were ruined. I hope he told her. And I hope that telling her gave him some moment of peace, and some sense of community with her, even if speaking about his assault also meant some crucial loss of control. I know that for me, as much as I regret publishing my book, I do not regret telling my mother, who never knew about my assault until my book's publication forced me, finally, to tell her. "I need to prepare you for what's coming," I said one night over dinner with her in a restaurant. My mother is a very tough person; she doesn't compliment, and she never cries. I remember she sat and listened to me, balling up her napkin as I told her, and then she cried.

And I remember the look on my ex's face when he told me what had been done to him. We were sitting outdoors in the grass at a concert, and he wouldn't look at me as he said it. The music thumped over and through his words. And yet I heard every syllable clearly, and with each word, some new detail about his face emerged for me. The exact outline of his ear, the fox-red hue of one corner of his beard. Minute by minute, my boyfriend became intensely *real* to me.

Perhaps that is the true value in giving our testimony: making us real to each other, not another figure in the grand political theater, not another sound bite on social media. And perhaps this, in the end, is why I am so angry about the book that I published: I never told my ex what had happened to me, not even after he told me about his rape. I told a thousand strangers for whom I have no actual meaning, who have no true meaning to me. I made myself a talking statistic for them, and refused to become truly real to a man who needed me.

My ex died two years ago without ever knowing my story. Had I told him when we were dating, perhaps I could have changed our relationship, changed his own relationship to himself, to his future wife, to his own body. But I was afraid then, and fear made me selfish. It was out of this sense of diminishment that I said nothing.

"Perhaps writers like us really can change the world," one young woman wrote me recently in a private Twitter message. "Your book inspired me to tell my own story. You can check out my feed." I sat and thumbed down the screen to read it, the image of this stranger, like me, humiliated and hurt, raw and furious, her own terrible story wedged now between video grabs from a Trump rally and a trailer for *John Wick 3*. I stopped reading and her story flickered past. I sent a message thanking her, adding a few glib notes of praise. I told her I hoped she'd continue writing. And then I deleted her message.

I Follow My Intuition

*

She unrolls like sharp and gold wire

toward decorous flowers.

I see the peach unmoving of them.

The family faces of them.

I hold a bouquet and push my face in the faces of roses.

Their childlike cheeks

satellite around me.

*

My father sanctions this tuberose carpet.

Who is the yellow bird that flies over?

Black arrows painted on ceremoniously on its wings.

Who is the bird?

*

Platinum fish fight through the sea

to have me / be had by me

I feel their involuntary muscles shatter the air.

I hide my fingernails.

I draw grass on the floor.

This isn't true..........

My father wasn't around.

For youuuuuuuuuuuuuuuuuuu…..

*

I drink an iceberg

Titter the aureole of

my incomprehension.

To hold the ponytail of

your roan body

lambasting across the capital

that hates you,

And yet,

*

My JOY

like aloe vera.

With her full arms.

Thanks me.

You're in the next room with our daughter.

Basil as grace notes,

feathers of basil in the strainer as

water searches through.

✻

I buy hats with brims

Then I black out

finking behind the berries.

✻

This isn't true……..

I wake up with "party bruises" on my head.

You can't be here when my roommates wake up.

You are like Galilee,

the reflection off Galilee when we gathered around

the alto,

the ring bearer.

We were marrying you.

You were marrying us.

✻

I told a bad joke

because I hated myself

but couldn't afford

the classroom of my hatred.

You took martini glasses away from me.

When you proposed, I remember only

the upthrust of my greasy fingers.

What happens to a "regular" person

shame-walking through Confederate memorials?

TBH: It feels like you said this before.

*

Must you always be looking

into the trunk of our car?

Sometimes people somersault into your garage.

Hold knives to your throat

and cut you.

When you are brown,

you are a gambler, madam.

*

Do you know the son

wilted down on the concrete.

We thought he was dead.

Mammals do that.

They can do death to survive.

*

It feels like I've seen this before,

like we've done this before.

*

Like some

some new Great Plains wind changing species

manipulating each state

spring

break.

A LOVE STORY

His Perfect Wife

She is tall and preferably white or, if an immigrant, not one who highlights the ills of America. She is able to endure physical labor of the sort required to perhaps chop wood, or haul sacks of earth or compost or branches, understands gardens and gardening, prefers decorative flowers to vegetables. She can upholster frayed seat covers. Or perhaps refurbish used furniture. She can strip and paint walls and fix things. Or, lacking those skills, has a deep appreciation for someone who possesses them.

She likes to run. Perhaps she is into American sports. Can name the winning ad during the Superbowl. Drinks beer.

She wears unfussy clothes and doesn't put a lot of thought into her appearance, but is attractive. She is tall and therefore has never had the need to put on heels and has made of this a virtue. She is given to looking askance at those who do, but only privately. It would not occur to her to be overtly cruel. She is gracious and her superiorities remain masked. She is earthy and has short hair. Or, if not, a haircut that stays out of the way. She is interested in weather patterns. She has a chest to write home about.

She likes to read, widely, and almost always only fiction. Together they disavow the inscrutability of poetry. The books between them accumulate, but only in their minds, not in their houses, and they discuss the ideas found in those books, the plant hardiness zone in the places where they build, renovate, and abandon homes, and the behavior of seasonal flora, on their walks. These conversations are intellectually pleasing, and they return home feeling freshly anointed by the intelligence and wit of the other.

Since he is, himself, a plant that thrives under careful circumstances, she is circumspect in how she expresses her love for him. She is at ease with distance, quiet, solitary pursuits, and steers clear of outbursts of any sort—about the weather, about the traffic, about politics—and under the careful light of her ambient unoppressive warmth he flourishes both at home and in the world. He embraces necessary and fulfilling work, so-far-and-no-further friendships, occasional forays into their peaceful community, and the raising of independent children. He is considered by all to be blessed and, in his good fortune, female strangers are comfortable telling him how lucky he is in his choice of life partner. This is also true for his perfect wife who is often regarded, by female friends and newly met acquaintances alike, as being fortunate in her choice of life-partner.

While other men admire him greatly for having her as a wife, she is not the kind of woman those men would wish were married to them. Other men never tell either of them that they are fortunate in their choices because she does not share that kind of emotional intimacy with anyone, and certainly not people of the opposite gender who round out her area of influence, and his circle of men all agree that if they were to say such a thing it would mean that they wanted to sleep with his wife and that is not an acceptable fantasy.

She never raises her voice. Fuck is not a word she would use if she's yelling at her kids. Then again she wouldn't be yelling at them so she wouldn't need the word *fuck*. Fucking in general won't be something she fancies. Actually, she has never fucked anybody in her life. She has only had sexual relations. This has not necessarily prevented them, as a couple, from enjoying regular and mutually satisfying expressions of physical intimacy.

She attends some, but not most of her children's activities. She would never fight coaches and school principals, let alone the superintendent. Those people wouldn't feel terrified when she walked into the room. People would respect her and like her, but never fear her, and this would be best for everyone, particularly The Extended Family.

She would be cognizant of what is going on in the world, but not feel she was in possession of the means to fix any ills except with regular checks to NPR, Amnesty International, the Red Cross, the ACLU, or, in a fit of real zeal, The Southern Poverty Law Center.

She would have the occasional dinner party and it contains a perfect meal that comes out of a cookbook or maybe *Cooking Light*, and she would be thought of as a gracious hostess. And though he misses the fire and spice lurking in every dish the imperfect wife cooks, he acknowledges that the polish and presentation of the soufflés and pies produced by his perfect wife are more universally craved by their friends (who only arrive when invited or with due and decent notice), and, indeed, countrymen, and his mind is eased.

She would love Thanksgiving and be a welcome addition to the family and it would be said of her, as it was once said of Ms. F_ , "she is a fine addition to the D_____family."

By the time she was fifty she'd wear twin-sets and sensible, but certainly well-made and fashionable, shoes. She would probably own clip-on earrings and these would never give her a headache. She'd have a solid job and a retirement plan. There would be no need to discuss money, but if the need arose to do so, it would be sensible.

They would be so content together, glad every day for the disasters they have avoided, the troubles they did not have to face—barring those ordinary ones of sickness and the passing away of relatives, the occasional errant child—and the great good fortune of having found such blissful stability, such solid gold good sense.

Instead, he has had to live with her. But she wonders, now, thinking about him, whether perhaps this is not true. That what he wanted was her, with the luxury fixings of all the things the dream woman is; the way you might buy a car with add-ons. Maybe he had only always wanted a vibrant, interesting female, but not one coveted by other men. Someone interested in the world but from behind the safe distance of newspapers and the vantage of armchairs. An engaged parent, but not an impulsive one. A competent appreciator of him.

This one, the one he married, lives alone.

Under cover of darkness, she writes an untitled poem for a man she won't name. A poem that nobody will ever read.

UNTITLED

Everything said about him is true

The curse of terrible regret makes ardor arduous
Poor translator confused by the peregrine's sorrow
he lives in his girded cage determined to outwit

love

Incapacitated to reach an inclement node clinging to another
season   make it flush green again   A confluence of lives
in concert play an unheard aria   He lets the petals drop

he does not he does not he does not

*

Her Perfect Husband

Has dark brown hair (because she is very far from the country that crowns its babies with the blue-black lush with which she is familiar), and eyes that can reflect the twin depths she carries beneath eyebrows no beautician can convince her to tame. He is tall enough to accommodate her preference for high heels which he admires without fail, as he admires the curve of her calf and the lift of her toes, and these things compel her to dress with specific intention toward his specific tastes, which shift easily to wrap around the shape she makes in the world.

He is wider and broader than she is, a frame that distinguishes her, and a solidity that protects her and in this regard he is, her perfect husband, much like the man for whom she is an imperfect wife. On the other hand, her perfect husband notes and admires her particular brilliance and commits himself to encouraging her to build her own frame, become her own protection in the world. He is thereby rewarded with a wife whom other men want for themselves but know they do not deserve.

He reads to understand not what has been written down, but what he is unable to articulate. For this reason, he is intimate with the way a poem both marks and carries a page forward into the void of his ignorance; how it finds and fills different blank spaces within him, leaving him simultaneously full and newly empty. He is wounded and healed by the written word and because he is, himself, clothed and iterated by words, he leaves no distance between the book he holds and his heart. This fragility does not require mending on her part. Their apartment fills up with books and friends who read and write them. Mostly poets.

In another life he picked flowers along the path to her house. In this life he brings her flowers from the grocery store, the farmer's market, and on occasion the florist, failing which he takes pictures of flowers for her to remind her that to him she is like a shrine at which he will place his offerings, faithful as any devotee at any temple in any country of the world.

He comes from a gregarious and messy family that is exceptionally clear about their affections, addictions, and ancestry, which can be traced back to cultures that favor food, family, gatherings—the larger the better—laughter, and the occasional story of revenge. His family is regularly bruised, composed of big dreams and average means, none of which prevents them from exuding a warmth that insists that the keys to their homes are duplicated often for the purpose of sharing.

When faced with the choice between the prudence of saving and the chaos of travel, he chooses travel. He is willing to accompany her to the museums, churches, and ruins that move her, though he does not feel compelled to absorb these things with the same intensity. In this latter regard, too, he is, her perfect husband, much like the man for whom she is an imperfect wife.

He may or may not like sports, but he joins in any she asks him to play. He is uninhibited which has the effect of drawing out a different creature from the contours of her mind and hence, her body. He places his palms on her belly emptied of children as though it is his privilege to touch the filigreed vase. He describes her such that she will consider his language the precise definition of her vastness and her limits. And though her sister-in-law had once said that she lived in the wrong country for American men coveted breasts and faces while her countrymen loved hair and arses, and though she will convey this to him, he will tell her how the precise measurement of her shoulders, wrists, waist, hips, fingers, feet, and breasts please him. Because his words move so close to his actions, because his hands are never far from her, it is easy to believe him.

He notes the attention that other men pay to her and is alternately amused or jealous, and both are conditions that he can share with her. Being of equal passion, their arguments are as heated as their agreement in the aftermath.

He lives with her silences but not so long that she forgets the way back home to him. He is unafraid of her moods and tempers. He threatens to smash the drunken face of a man who throws a stray comment at their lust in passing, with the bottle he holds in his hand. He says *I'm done with you* and *don't leave me* in the same conversation. He can drink too much and not drink at all. He can chain-smoke or quit altogether. He can sleep all day and stay out all night. He likes to spend his time only with her but also at a dance club or gatherings where only one of them is known or neither is, but where the food and wine and talk are good. This makes him not one man but many, a quality that suits a complex woman with a fairly insatiable appetite for change and devotion.

His photographs of her capture her in ways nobody has seen. In each she is lit from within. He finds her beautiful and tells her so.

He is careful to stay on the outside when they walk, usually in big cities or foreign ones, which makes her feel seen and watched over. He notices if she is cold or drunk, and offers his jacket or his care accordingly. His awareness of her is vital to her. He understands that if it falters, she will drift away.

Her perfect husband does not fix anything, haul lumber, demolish and rebuild houses, dismantle and reassemble various pieces of equipment from computer printers to cars. He does not run a marathon or climb a mountain or set up camp or drive a stick-shift on the winding roads of the Italian coast without denting the rental car. He does not predict the weather day after day, give her the roadmap for her journeys along the highways of America, or hang a painting. He does not juggle, play baseball, and tennis, or ski down the mountains of Aspen, Breckenridge, Loveland, Telluride, and Silverton or, to put it in numbers, down mountains ranging from 12,510 feet to 13,487 feet. He does not navigate a sailboat, build a campfire, or scale a ladder bearing an 11x7 foot triple-glazed, high solar-gain, low-E pane of glass to install in a second floor bedroom of his own design.

Her perfect husband does not pick up and hold fully-grown daughters above his head to throw them into deep waters around her island country, or to place angels on the tops of Christmas trees that scratch the many roofs that shelter them in America. They are not his to hold.

In these significant ways the perfection of her perfect husband is diminished until she remembers that both husbands are untrue things born of circumstance and yearning.

Under cover of darkness she writes a titled poem for the man she names. A poem that can do no harm. Or so she likes to believe, driving the unsheathed sword bought for dancing, the one beneath which she had learned to spin, deep into her own heart. She thinks of this as a necessary repair.

POEM FOR OTHER MEN

You, whose glance remains tangled in duplicity   entranced
        you do not love her.

You do not love her who have never seen her walk

naked   virginal through the laid paths of a Carolina trail
or lain in the dunes of Truro with a small fire
        duly permitted by the law
                confiding the entirety of a family's history
                        not a confession but a lifting of burdens
You do not love her who never led bare feet over
the fanged heights that skirt the far Northern
edges of your country nor ever used the lit end of sticks
        to show her what she was destined to doubt:
                a nation's celebration of war renamed for freedom
                        your childlike joy taking flight
                                beside a bear-threatened campsite
but only after drinking coffee she offers from the first-aid kit
packed to save her from America   A black brew pure
going down hard announcing that   she   like the culture that raised her
will always take her time   she   will bring a bitter warmth,
        what sweetness is required must come whole
                tasted   with a tongue licking
                        the surface of her bowl-shaped palm
You do not love her who never saw the jewel at the back of the thrift store
did not pick her off her feet & carry her home dressed in pink

cotton and lace bought off the sale rack at the Salvation Army

nor brave the ridicule of your friends to say out loud to this brown-

    girl-in-the-ring who never dressed as others did

        no   not even then

                I came to see you dance last night

You do not love her who have not watched her spin

in the arms of other men under the chandelier prisms

of a ballroom in years after and later still sat by the fire

house quiet as she danced for you losing zills from her fingers jeweled

    scarf from her hips   spun silver sword from her head

        moving

                to the sound of your breath and hers

You do not love her who have not held her leaning

into the punk stink of a gritty taxi already laboring to rent a car

at a city airport   too young to know better nor watched her

in the hours to come terrified that the life

    looking for light will be replacement

        not gift

You do not love her who have not fed her the right thing

nor played the wrong music—James Brown—nor felt

in that luckless wake the force of her desperation

You do not love her who have not watched her run

    in socks on ice nor combed each matted strand

        her hair unbound in adolescent unknowing

            nor washed the skeined skin

                that prevents her escape

You do not love her who have not held an infant turning blue

who have not stood before her helpless and uttered the unsayable:

I cannot save her   who have not seen her turn to seek a power

beyond anything you could ever offer

    who do not know what fragile joy returns

        with the returned child

You do not love her who have neither seen nor denied

the acuminous sadness she carries   its weight your weight

weightless and moving deep and further from you

who have not listened to statements of endings   collected

    broken chairs & table overturned nor felt relief

        that an ocean crashing over her island

            could make her whole

You do not love her who have not picked from the floor the knife

shard of blue   fragment of art   gifted at marriage broken

in the aftermath of a fight begun over Bergman's best intentions

You do not love her who have not fallen in love with her singing

voice the   sway of her body & watched both crumble nor

    witnessing each determined renewal

        reached for the filigreed vase

You do not love her who have not known the depths of her friendships

slate springs before which she kneels to slake unquenchable thirsts

nor waited in patience for the end of her journeys

for the faithful heart and what comes with its jagged borders

    spoken words flung   the soothe of lullabies sung

        to daughters each according to taste

            and tolerance for love expressed

You do not love her who have not lain through the dark night in silence

who have not felt the vastness of the spilled space left uncrossed between
who have not   in the deepest sleep still unfurled your fingers
and taken the hand placed in yours   You do not love her
who do not know all this   all this   and this   too
    You do not love her who do not know
            This is the measure of love.

*

Their perfect spouses only love the woman and man they see and know, whole and beautiful and theirs. She does not get to be his wife. He does not get to be her husband. Their perfect husband and wife marry other people and become those people's imperfect husband and wife and in this way all four, cut from the same cloth, are subject to the same heartache. In separate parts of the world, or maybe the country, or even the same town, that cloth tares and they weep without witness.

*

As pointed out by Atwood, whether it is A, B, C, D, E, or F, all love stories end the same way. In some traditions this is seen as relief.

Detroit

I woke up in a hot room in Detroit
after pushing two fingers into my vagina
and hooking them into your memory:
lips, tongue, and jaw.
Sometimes I picture my fishbowl
mouth drinking up your body,
you, spit and collateral damage—
your father's ghost, fleshy
and good-humored, eating at a table
with you, post-apocalypse, then you
waking up with tears, feeling stunned.
I am 3,000 miles away. I cannot put
my hand over your heart,
that softest spot on your chest,
which I once pressed my lips hard into.
I touch the computer keys
and you touch your computer keys
and we transmit messages
I say, You are your father, spectral light,
hologram. I say, you are eros pulsing
on the horizon, the flicker of stars,
and between my legs, a light which

waxes and wanes—a lightning
bug, a desk lamp, such rare
incandescence. Did I tell you that
my father was a soldier, that twelve
years swallowed him up? Can
you feel your uncle's absence
flickering? Tonight, the LED lights
are scattered on the floor. Your mouth
painted stars onto my body.
Where your tongue tip touched,
a constellation lit up.

Tender

"Get the fuck out of my house," she said levelly. Asperger conspired with Nazis. Your misunderstanding of this episode brought to you by the Third Reich . . .

"You're just a dumb nigger."

SPECTRUM. "Get the fuck—." He had already gone, jerking the kitchen door shut behind him. She stood at the door staring toward the street, but her eyes drifted immediately. Not to the empty quiet place outside where he had driven away in his pickup, but to a copse of trees she knew thirty miles outside of town, the spot in the woods where she had first suspected him tender. Drift.

I'm 'on find me a razor blade and lay Reuben in the shade, start me a graveyard of my own.

Oh me, oh Lordy, my. Start me a graveyard of my own.

At night, when the light's on in the kitchen, the window in the kitchen door becomes a mirror.

He scuttled, shoving the last of his clothes into an old military surplus duffel bag, down the kitchen steps toward the truck. EPISODE: a flat green cue card with white lettering in her mind. She might have laughed, except the doppelgänger added, "You're dead. You're fucking dead."

She might have laughed.

Even the cursor gets lost when it hits the doppelgänger. How do you parse that? An unmarked spot on the page where the flashing stops. The whole line disappears. You're left. In a borderless area. A site you want to label 1944 regardless however nothing's for you there. Nothing safe for you regardless however here the walls have fallen. Find the pediatrician and maybe you can get somewhere. Blink, blink, blink. The cursor's the edge of an open door. Then it's gone.

Later when she sees herself reflected in the closed door, she'll recognize the room. "Fi?" She'll ask her mirrored self, "Fiona?"

"You're so stupid; when the fascists come they're going to kill you first."

Ol' Reuben made a train, he put it on a track, and he ran it to the Lord knows where.

Oh me, oh Lordy my, he ran it to the Lord knows where.

She'd followed him deep into the pines. "Les, where are we going?" He had not smiled but she'd been able to tell by the way he carried himself that he was pleased, by his determined stride ahead of her in the forest; by the way he rubbed his hands together. Stimming. Fiona tapped her chin, mouthed the lyrics of an old-time tune on repeat. She loved the smell of the pine trees, the cushiony feel of the fallen needles under her hiking boots, how they made an umber carpet almost the same color as his beard.

"I love it out here."

"We used to play back here all the time when I was a kid," Les had said.

"It's so soft." She'd stomped the ground, then hopped once. Then again. A little hop.

"The mycelium's pulling energy from our footsteps," he'd said.

"Say mycelium again and watch what happens."

Something about his eyes reminded her of a bird of prey. They flashed green and watchful. "Your eyes twinkle when you're happy," she'd said. She'd reached up to scratch his beard and he'd hugged her, wrapping her for a moment in his camouflage army jacket. Drift.

How had people who'd escaped from slavery done it? Fiona glanced back over her shoulder. No trail, no visible path revealed the route they'd just taken from Les's father's cabin. They'd gone far enough that the house was no longer visible. She could not escape a long history of the need for escape, never felt far enough removed. Strange in 2017, though not strange enough. She had not shared the thought with Les. He'd marched ahead of her through the forest. Had they lived in a different time, could he have been someone she trusted?

What made him someone she could trust in 2017? She'd met him two years ago in the garden section at Agway, where he'd been buying plants for a customer's garden project. She'd felt drawn to him because he cared for plants and trees. In the woods, he'd stopped and turned to wait for her. She'd tripped over a root and she'd caught him giving her a look he often levelled at her lately, as if he were surprised she'd survived her own life for this long. His eyes had narrowed like a hawk's. She'd read no bemusement on his face. Only concern, concentration. Had she seen a tinge of anger? Turning aside, he'd gestured with his chin. "Look." There decaying in the forest sat a '56 Cadillac Fleetwood Sixty Special.

My love, my love, what have I done to make you treat me so?
You caused me to weep. You caused me to moan.
You caused me to leave my home . . .

You're between periods. Snagged in a set of lyrics, you lament. A set of imperatives cost lives. Call them 1944. You must delineate, not hint at history. Else what? Of your life?

"You are the WORST person I have ever been with, and that's saying something!"

Fiona recognizes the world she spies in the kitchen door reflection as somewhere inaccessible, the woman she sees there—impossibly younger-looking, long-lashed and doe-eyed, eyebrows raised slightly in an expression of surprise—how had that hapless woman indeed not found herself the subject of some regrettable, forgettable headline? A banal and violent tragedy? A disappearance? " . . . *the colors and the lines that trace the past / will in the semidarkness form a face . . .*"

"*For once, then, something.*" Lines from two poems, the first, Borges, the second, Frost, occur to her, and for the umpteenth time she makes a mental note: replace the door with a Dutch door that will open at the top while remaining shut at the bottom. And for the umpteenth time, just after, she feels a shiver of dread at the thought of a bird flying into the house. A bad omen. She opens the refrigerator and stares blankly at the contents of that lit-up little box. How had she fallen in love with death?

"What in the world?" she had asked Les, marveling at the car. "How?" The pine forest seemed too dense for anyone to have driven the Fleetwood to the spot where it rested.

"Some old guy running from the law back then. He built this cabin"— Les had nodded toward a small, square, well-built one-room shack nearby—"and never left."

The little cabin itself had seemed almost to disappear into the surroundings. One could have stumbled upon it before even noticing it. The rusting car had retained its elegant lines and great bright swaths of its color: Orion Blue. Fiona had wondered whether the spray of perfectly round rust markings on the trunk had come from bullet holes, or if instead, somehow, the natural process of decay had simply progressed like that, advancing via dark, orange-rimmed, ever-widening hungry circles.

"I read an article once about a Mafia sting that happened near here in the fifties," she'd said. Les had squinted at her, scowling watchfully. Drift. Remember how to get here, remember, she had thought to herself, as though her own life or others' might someday depend upon it.

She wrapped her arms around him beneath his jacket. "Oh no! The snuggle tree has got me!" Les feigned resistance as Fiona pressed her head against his chest. "Oh no! Oh no!" he cried in a high, creaking voice. "The snuggle tree is blossoming . . . !" Cue: EPISODE. The doppelgänger draws a thumb slowly, silently across a throat.

"You're dead. You're fucking dead."

In 1944, you find Asperger and the words *racial hygiene*. Describe an absence becoming acutely your own. Struggle to cohere. As he struggles, in 2017, she struggles. A cursory description. A cursor. Now curse. Maybe you are curious, but those two: they want to drive away.

Black girl, black girl, don't lie to me.
Where did you sleep last night?

In the pines, in the pines, where the sun never shines
and you shiver when the cold wind blows.

What would stop her from disappearing? In the mirror night makes of the kitchen door's window, she finds herself always wrong to the light.

The pediatrician Asperger practiced, in 1944, what he called "pedagogical optimism." The fuck? Now that's out in the open. Decide what to do with it. Will you give it to the chorus? Bury it in a dialogue that's sung? What were they trying to say to each other before the doppelgänger arrived? How would you pronounce the impossibility that haunted them? How they saw the living ghost of love, saw themselves as wraiths? Sing it. Teach them what they should do.

She had slammed the door and for a second found herself separated from the doppelgänger by glass, staring into that uncanny face. There had been a flicker. She had thought for a moment she saw Les, her Les, again, but in a twinkling his features had crumpled, then set into the doppelgänger's mask of contempt. She could hear him still, barking insults, but she had turned away, thrown herself down into the beaten-down green armchair in the living room. EPISODE: the cue card had flashed in her mind. Her eyes had already drifted, other-placing.

The sounds of the key in the lock, the doorknob turning, were so familiar; at first, she did not register them, ascribed to them no meaning. Then suddenly he was in the kitchen again. "The fuck!—" she sprang by instinct from the chair, disoriented, not so much frightened as stunned. How had he—?

"You can't even drink this!"

"You don't need this so I'm taking it."

Ol' Reuben had a wreck 'n broke his fuckin' neck his
poor body never was found.
They found his head in a drivin' wheel
mile and half out of town.

Les had opened the refrigerator and yanked out a gallon of milk. Gripping it tightly in his fist, he had held it aloft in front of her like a trophy, like a threat.

Night falls and Fiona catches herself humming, glimpses herself alone, though she stands in the exact place where Les had stood that afternoon, having reappeared suddenly before her like a specter. Had his fingers transformed into talons? His auburn hair to feathers? Had he torn the carton apart in a single gesture, sending a violent white splash and spray of milk across the appliances and linoleum, across the stainless surface of the refrigerator and glass of the kitchen door's window, she could not have found him as strange as she found her own face.

She had not known what to call it. For it had not been a coherent thought. Just a sense of something broader under the joy she had felt with him. Love. Spent. She had recognized him as fugitive. The way she recognized herself. And he had given her the car. A memorable moving gift. But neither could say how they knew that day: they had escaped nothing. Something history owed they would need to pay.

"What if I really turned into a tree right now?" she had asked.

"I'd perch right up here in your leaves," he had said, gathering her braids together into a crown. "And when it came time to die, I'd lie down right here and decompose and feed your roots."

"I'd know all the tree gossip," she'd said as he bit at the knot of braids he'd made as though he would gobble her up hair first. "I could tell you what really went down out here."

"I'd already know," he'd said. "I'd be part of it, part of what told you, part of what you'd tell."

How they run their fingers over the surfaces of their lives, hoping the cursor will reappear. She told you to get the fuck out! But you assumed. You assumed she was talking to him.

She might have laughed.

"You can't even drink this!"

Is there a doctor in the house?

Well, you shoulda been in town when ol' Reuben's train went down
You could hear that whistle blow 100 miles
Oh me, oh Lordy my, hear that whistle blow 100 miles.

She closes the door as night falls, the tune steady running through her mind. She sings it all to the tear-stained face she sees.

So much for 1944, for 2017. So much for the getaway. For the vehicle stashed so long it's gone to seed: a car that feels so meant for you when you happen upon its slow decay, you wonder if it wasn't you that secreted it there—*in the pines, in the pines . . .*

—May Loufoque
2019

Death of a Family

I.

When did we become mortal enemies? You campaigned early and hard to be our heroine and for a while it worked. But you weren't entertaining any questions. Who besides poets have studied the intimacies of violence and lies? I hear it's cold in heaven and getting colder—inversely proportionate to the warming on earth. The seraphim—bless their souls—are busy burning the documents of the saved. But still no damn heat. You claimed to defy heat like that nineteenth-century Indian princess—she of the silk brocades and stately elephants—who on sultry days teleported herself to the Himalayas.

A good daughter never speaks of the savagery of mothers.

II.

How many did you send? Fifty? One hundred? Thank-you cards to the parents who wish you dead? Subjugation junkie. Holy broken body. There's no end to your tasks. Stop. It's your last moment alive. Then poof, you're gone. What do you say?

III.

Forget your tin scepter. Your baroque concealments. The frail men in your basement bathing hamsters and cooking you colonial meals. Everything around us degrades, sister. Time will steal what remains. Overhead the ex-gods cast their shrinking shadows. No amnesty for the unrepentant, I say. You disagree. We no longer fit in the same life. But in the next one, why not be ordinary sinners together? And I, for one, will speak Polish.

IV.

Soon you'll be dead but I'm done grieving the younger you. Between here and there, then and now, you missed the wild light. Life received you in a thatch hut on stilts. You identified river snakes by their slither and gleam. Peed through the wooden slats into the turbid waters, marking nothing. Because nothing had been taken from you yet. Now your spine crumbles from the unceasing labor of being right. You might live longer without memories but may I remind you of the time you cut my steak into tiny pieces long after I could cut it myself? What's the opposite of a nocturne? A daydream?

Empire-Building Requires Ruthlessness

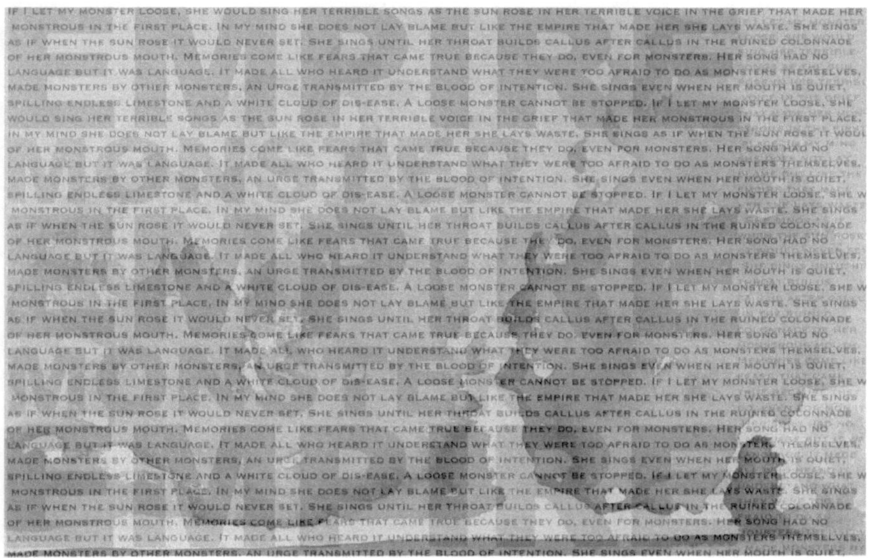

If I let my monster loose, she would sing her terrible songs a
monstrous in the first place. In my mind she does not lay blam
as if when the sun rose it would never set. She sings until he
of her monstrous mouth. Memories come like fears that came t
language but it was language. It made all who heard it unders
made monsters by other monsters, an urge transmitted by the
spilling endless limestone and a white cloud of dis-ease. A lo
would sing her terrible songs as the sun rose in her terrible
in my mind she does not lay blame but like the empire that mad
of her monstrous mouth. Memories come like fears that came t
language but it was language. It made all who heard it unders
made monsters by other monsters, an urge transmitted by the
spilling endless limestone and a white cloud of dis-ease. A lo
monstrous in the first place. In my mind she does not lay blam
as if when the sun rose it would never set. She sings until he
of her monstrous mouth. Memories come like fears that came t
language but it was language. It made all who heard it unders
made monsters by other monsters, an urge transmitted by the
spilling endless limestone and a white cloud of dis-ease. A lo
monstrous in the first place. In my mind she does not lay blam
as if when the sun rose it would never set. She sings until he
of her monstrous mouth. Memories come like fears that came t
language but it was language. It made all who heard it unders
made monsters by other monsters, an urge transmitted by the
spilling endless limestone and a white cloud of dis-ease. A lo
monstrous in the first place. In my mind she does not lay blam
as if when the sun rose it would never set. She sings until he
of her monstrous mouth. Memories come like fears that came t
language but it was language. It made all who heard it unders
made monsters by other monsters, an urge transmitted by the
spilling endless limestone and a white cloud of dis-ease. A lo
monstrous in the first place. In my mind she does not lay blam
as if when the sun rose it would never set. She sings until he
of her monstrous mouth. Memories come like fears that came t
language but it was language. It made all who heard it unders
made monsters by other monsters, an urge transmitted by the

S THE SUN ROSE IN HER TERRIBLE VOICE IN THE GRIEF THAT MADE HER
ME BUT LIKE THE EMPIRE THAT MADE HER SHE LAYS WASTE. SHE SINGS
R THROAT BUILDS CALLUS AFTER CALLUS IN THE RUINED COLONNADE
RUE BECAUSE THEY DO, EVEN FOR MONSTERS. HER SONG HAD NO
TAND WHAT THEY WERE TOO AFRAID TO DO AS MONSTERS THEMSELVES,
BLOOD OF INTENTION. SHE SINGS EVEN WHEN HER MOUTH IS QUIET,
OSE MONSTER CANNOT BE STOPPED. IF I LET MY MONSTER LOOSE, SHE
VOICE IN THE GRIEF THAT MADE HER MONSTROUS IN THE FIRST PLACE.
E HER SHE LAYS WASTE. SHE SINGS AS IF WHEN THE SUN ROSE IT WOUL
RUE BECAUSE THEY DO, EVEN FOR MONSTERS. HER SONG HAD NO
TAND WHAT THEY WERE TOO AFRAID TO DO AS MONSTERS THEMSELVES,
BLOOD OF INTENTION. SHE SINGS EVEN WHEN HER MOUTH IS QUIET,
OSE MONSTER CANNOT BE STOPPED. IF I LET MY MONSTER LOOSE, SHE W
ME BUT LIKE THE EMPIRE THAT MADE HER SHE LAYS WASTE. SHE SINGS
R THROAT BUILDS CALLUS AFTER CALLUS IN THE RUINED COLONNADE
RUE BECAUSE THEY DO, EVEN FOR MONSTERS. HER SONG HAD NO
TAND WHAT THEY WERE TOO AFRAID TO DO AS MONSTERS THEMSELVES,
BLOOD OF INTENTION. SHE SINGS EVEN WHEN HER MOUTH IS QUIET,
OSE MONSTER CANNOT BE STOPPED. IF I LET MY MONSTER LOOSE, SHE W
ME BUT LIKE THE EMPIRE THAT MADE HER SHE LAYS WASTE. SHE SINGS
R THROAT BUILDS CALLUS AFTER CALLUS IN THE RUINED COLONNADE
RUE BECAUSE THEY DO, EVEN FOR MONSTERS. HER SONG HAD NO
TAND WHAT THEY WERE TOO AFRAID TO DO AS MONSTERS THEMSELVES,
BLOOD OF INTENTION. SHE SINGS EVEN WHEN HER MOUTH IS QUIET,
OSE MONSTER CANNOT BE STOPPED. IF I LET MY MONSTER LOOSE, SHE W
ME BUT LIKE THE EMPIRE THAT MADE HER SHE LAYS WASTE. SHE SINGS
R THROAT BUILDS CALLUS AFTER CALLUS IN THE RUINED COLONNADE
RUE BECAUSE THEY DO, EVEN FOR MONSTERS. HER SONG HAD NO
TAND WHAT THEY WERE TOO AFRAID TO DO AS MONSTERS THEMSELVES,
BLOOD OF INTENTION. SHE SINGS EVEN WHEN HER MOUTH IS QUIET.

Untitled Excerpt

Innocent stood in the middle of the trailer; the children crowded together in the back. The four of them were cramped, it was the smallest trailer on the carnival's lot, but it couldn't be helped. At least it would be easier to stay warm. As it was, the bar of lye soap froze to Innocent's hand now and again. He couldn't get the stove to stay lit. He talked to the children as he worked, just nonsense, just any old thing to fill the silence.

"Manager said we going down to Texas. We supposed to be on our way down there right now, 'Crawfish come November,' Manager said. And he went on about what a crawfish look like. Like none of us ever saw nothing but these Oklahoma plains. I been down Texas. I seen plenty of water . . ." He paused and shook his head at a memory he didn't want to have.

"You remember your ma?" Innocent asked, turning to May. She wriggled beneath the blanket Innocent had just laid over her.

"I do. I remember your ma."

May's mouth opened in its enormous and incredible O; her single long tooth caught the light of the gas lantern and shined a milky amber. Pretty. Like an icicle hanging from the eave of a cave. Innocent thought he might like to have it—afterward. He fished his good-luck marble from his pocket and put it in May's hand. Her mouth widened till it was as big as a hippo's mouth: May's Incredible Maw was how they billed her.

"That's yours, May," he said. "This way we each have something of the other's to keep."

She smiled at him with her little bitty squirrel eyes and he squeezed her hand as he moved away from her to check the stove.

Innocent had brought in plenty of wood, but the half-frozen twigs hissed when he put a flame to them and wouldn't catch. He had a pail of water he'd brought in for the children's baths—a film of ice glassed the surface of the water and shattered each time Innocent dipped the rag and soap. He had already bathed three of them, there was only Honey left.

"I'm sorry," he said as he unbuttoned her dress. The water was so cold Innocent lost sensation in his fingers, the nails had purpled. He rubbed the stiffening rag between the folds of fat on Honey's thigh. The swells and lumps and rolls of her shook under his ministrations, the expanse of her belly was ridged with goose bumps. Honey didn't scream or squirm, she only cried big round tears that welled over the slits of her eyelids and ran down her cheeks and quivering triple chin.

"Cold, Inny," she said. Because this cold was cruel and stinging and because she couldn't imagine why he was rubbing her with this rag that hurt her—he had never hurt any of them.

"Soon be over," Innocent said. "But y'all got to be clean. Everything clean."

The rest of them, those that could talk—that is to say all but May—joined in.

"Inny, Inny. Fire please."

The oldest of them was only ten, and they were simple, all of them simple in the head, which made it worse to see them suffer.

"I know," Innocent said. "I know. But y'all can't make a fuss or you'll wake up the whole camp."

He peered through the hole he'd made in the newspaper covering the trailer's single window. It was true what Ava said, how they set up the living lot the same way everywhere they stopped, with their trailers positioned in straight intersecting lines like a street grid in a city. Ava had even drawn a map and named the imaginary streets. She had wanted to put up house numbers too, hung on shingles in each trailer's doorway, but Manager had said that was too much, and he gave one of his speeches about carnival life and how it was their blessing that they weren't yolked to any towns or street names or five-and-dimes, or to the people in them. *We are the light*, Manager said—can't cover it up with regular people–type shit.

"Fire!" Honey said.

Innocent rushed to the stove. The weight of their situation suddenly impressed itself upon him—the biting cold, the lateness of the hour, the children's exhaustion—they had worked that night, a little while anyway, before the cold came down, and there were so few people on the midway that Manager shut the show down for the night. The children had not had their supper. Joli was crabbed in the corner, tottering on a chair far too small for him. He had shot up to six foot five in the last month and he was only nine years old. His growing pains were worse in the cold.

"Babies!" Innocent said, addressing all four of the children. Joli, beginning to cry, pressed the palms of his hands against his eye sockets—his fingers stuck straight up and were so wide and long and crooked that he looked as though he'd grown antlers.

"Babies!" Innocent said again. His hands shook on the wooden matches. One by one they broke as he tried to light them. The matchbox emptied until there was only one. The sparking head splintered off from the stick and fell, as the others had, into the black belly of the stove.

"Babies," he said again. His voice was shrill. Behind him, Innocent's children waited in silence. Their eight eyes were on him. He glanced back at them and in that instant he was one of them—that helpless, that cast away. How had he become the one who was supposed to take care of them when he was just as pitiful as they were? He'd give anything to have Ava back. All of this mess and trouble they were in and it was up to him to fix it—a nobody from nowhere. He couldn't do it. He didn't have the courage.

Even now, out there in the dark rows of the living lot, out on the midway, his friends, his colleagues and comrades, people he had loved, were plotting against him. He could hear their treachery skittering around in their heads like big black beetles. They wanted shut of him. They wanted to demote him to shoveling horseshit. And his babies, Innocent's babies they wanted to chuck by the roadside like sick dogs. A month ago they'd been clapping Innocent on the back and calling him brother. *How far we fell*, Innocent thought.

No telling now what he might do. There wasn't any defense against them, Innocent's babies couldn't run or fight. They didn't have the slightest inkling of the plot against them. How they trusted Innocent, despite the shivering and hunger and exhaustion; they trusted that he would find another book of matches and make a fire and then he'd tuck blankets around them and they'd all go to sleep and wake to porridge and bacon as they had all of their other mornings. They trusted him to make it so because he loved them. With him they were safe. Even on nights when townies crowded into the sideshow tents on the midway, when they jeered and shoved each other for a better look at whichever of Innocent's babies were onstage. When they shouted and called them aberrations and freaks. When they looked at May and said she wasn't anything God had made. When they threw peanuts, and sticks from which they'd sucked off the cotton candy. When they tossed, as they had one time, a rock that hit Honey on the forehead and she'd had to stay onstage under the hot lights, blinking against the blood trickling into her eyes. Oh, but, when the show was over, there was Innocent. Always. He hefted her into her wheelbarrow and maneuvered her offstage and down the midway to his trailer where he cleaned the wound with a warm cloth and rubbed it with a salve that took the sting out. He propped her head in his lap and whispered in her ear, *Brave and sweet and wasn't nobody like her on all the earth.* He whispered these things only to her. He rested his chin in her palm so she could run her fingers over his prickly beard, and if she sometimes pinched or slapped him—because sometimes there wasn't anything else to do in a world like this—Inny didn't hit her back or even chastise. He loved her, Honey knew, and no one else ever had.

Innocent kneeled on the floor next to the stove. "Babies!" His voice was only a whisper, hushed with futility. And he was sorry, so very sorry. He rose to his haunches and spread his arms wide. The children thought it was an embrace and were comforted.

"Y'all ain't never seen the ocean," he said.

The place where Innocent was born was menaced by a violent and unpredictable sea. For a string of days it would be passive, friendly even, and the people of Innocent's town ventured out in little boats or if the weather was warm they'd hike up their pants and skirts and wade in to their knees. Then, without any warning, or so it seemed to Innocent as a boy, the sea turned mean and charged up onto the shore with murder in its heart. It battered the people until there wasn't anything left but wood splinters where houses should have been—and the weeping women and stone-faced men staring out to the horizon. It was at the onset of one of these storms that Innocent, stepping through the pine brake that ringed the beach, found his father standing at the edge of the shore, the waves breaking around him. His arms were spread wide, as Innocent's arms were spread now as he kneeled in front of his babies. He wasn't more than six or seven at the time, and he thought that perhaps his father was telling the sea that he loved it, so that it would be kind to Innocent and his parents and their flimsy house rocking into the wind. In the next instant, his father leaned into the oncoming waves, arms still spread wide, and was carried out into the depths.

All his life, Innocent had judged his father a weak man and a coward. But now, looking out at the children, he understood that his father had simply surrendered. Death and the water were bound to win sooner or later. Innocent sighed, got to his feet, and did what needed doing.

"Supper! Supper!" Honey said. Innocent had taken a tin of potato mash from his satchel and was spooning it into Honey's mouth. The food was cold and there was a bitter aftertaste, but she liked the bits of chopped bacon. He fed them all in turn, everybody's favorite, with the Barbies mixed in.

VENTRILOQUIST MUSEUM

In the Vent Haven Ventriloquist Museum in Fort Mitchell, Kentucky, she realizes she is ruined for meat.

The person she loves doesn't eat it and what if they kiss? She wants to be pure in her mouth.

Vent Haven has four puppets that visitors may handle to try their hand at ventriloquism, but the remainder of the exhibits are not for handling. Parents may want to consider if children under age seven are old enough to enjoy the museum.

The collection began when William Shakespeare Berger purchased his first figure, Tommy Baloney, in 1910. Then he purchased another. And another. One open mouth asked for another and another until four rooms of his house were full of open mouths.

He married, had a son, and that son had a son, but still William Shakespeare Berger did not want his vast collection of dummies to be scattered or thrown away. So many puppets and no more hands to fill them. Tommy Baloney's face was full of nicks and smudges and greasy fingerprints by this time. William Shakespeare Berger wanted his puppets to be safe.

So many mouths said: *Oh.*

In Kentucky, you can find Confederate flags displayed on a car window. In Connecticut, you can find Confederate flags hung over a garage. On mugs, on t-shirts, bumper stickers. Even on a neckerchief for a dog. It is 2019 and if you still don't get that displaying a Confederate flag— the flag of people who wanted to keep black people slaves—you're just a crackalacka treasonous person. Or probably named Chad. Shut your piehole about heritage. If you love to display the Confederate flag, surprise: your heritage is HATE!

Let so many mouths never eat what used to have breath. Let them kiss and kiss and be pure and say only: *Oh.*

SPINAL COLUMN

Black women are supposed to have strong backbones but my Black back is jacked.

Before he cracked my neck, the chiropractor told me I had an Atlas tilt at the top of my cervical spine. The weight of the world on my shoulders. It was unclear to me whether the Atlas could be manipulated back into place on its axis.

Ori mi pe, the classic Adire cloth indigo design, literally translates as, "my head is correct." In Yoruba belief the head is the seat of personal destiny. Therefore, *ori mi pe* means, "I will have a good destiny." But my head is not correct. The junction of my skull and spine is off, the nerve center misfiring in that cathedral of delicate bones. I wonder what this means about my destiny.

When did I start feeling the pain? I think it was when our republic elected the demagogue. I remember the presidential debate. She, in her white pantsuit. He, pacing behind her like a menacing ape. The familiarity of that dance. He's going to hit her, I thought. I clenched my shoulders. I have not been able to unclench them since.

The election coincided with a great heartbreak of which I dare not speak, even with a facsimile of anonymity. The heartache would fall to others, like a chain of dominoes, wrecking multiple lives. I would rather carry the grief alone. It is enough to say that the external calamity, which was political, coincided with the internal calamity, which was personal. My body, my country: broken.

Cervix refers to the neck, or any neck-like part, especially the constricted lower end of the uterus.

When he was deep inside me, my lover, my predator, claimed that he could feel my cervix.

"Do you feel guilty?" asked the primary care physician before referring me to a psychotherapist. I was already seeing a therapist, who'd insisted on blood work and recommended bringing my husband to vouch for the truth of my pain since doctors, as a general rule, disbelieve women. My husband was busy. I was busier than him by far, and on top of that, I was sick. The blood test could not explain why my hair was falling out. Thyroid, endocrine system, hormones: normal range. And yet,

I could barely get out of bed. I wasn't free to stay in bed. Duty called. My children needed food and feeding, washing, cuddles, stories, protection from the incessant evil messaging of white folks, and lotion on their ashy knees. My students needed feedback, mentoring, encouragement, recommendation letters, and advice on handling the sexual advances of their male professors. My health insurance needed explanations for all the office visits. Either my spine was the sum of my moods or a vertical timeline of historical abuse.

The orthopedic surgeon barely glanced at the x-rays before accusing me of being a boring patient. "You must have a lot of time on your hands," he dismissed my symptoms, "to be worrying over nothing." The pain, he implied, was all in my head. I did not have a lot of time on my hands. I had next to no time to myself, practically none at all. But it felt as though I was suffering whiplash. I am the backbone of my family, I wanted to tell him, *how dare you speak to me like that*, I am the backbone of my community. I am an educated woman suffering private heartache under a dictatorship.

The symptoms radiating down the nervous system like falling dominoes included tension headache, jaw pain, limited head rotation, stiff neck, shoulder pain, tennis elbow, carpal tunnel syndrome, pelvic asymmetry, asthma, protrusion of disks, chronically cold hands and feet, low blood pressure, low self-confidence, chronic diarrhea, despair, and fatigue. Worst of all, I could no longer hold up my head.

The dentist said I was like the princess and the pea. My teeth conveyed no rationale for the throbbing pain in my jaw. He accused my mouth of perfect teeth but nevertheless referred me to an oral surgeon with the manner of a Nazi. I told him I couldn't sleep. You're like the princess and the pea, the surgeon said, with the same disdain as the dentist. The two of them were in a private club, they shared a language, a philosophy predicated on the put-down. Neither man would prescribe painkillers. In spite of my straight white teeth, they suspected that I was an addict hustling for opiates, that my mouth was a den of lies.

The pain travelled. While I searched for care, countless women, including my mother, gathered in the cities, and in the capital, and across the globe, wearing pink pussy hats. Meanwhile, my husband asked me to leave our apartment so that he could play violent video games in solitude. "Call of Duty." He was granted an award for being a genius. When the school complained about the behavior of our son, it was me they called, never him.

I was not alone in my illness, nor alone in being blamed for my illness. We grew fibroids. Nobody knew why more black and brown women were afflicted at a higher rate. Our uterine lining began appearing in unexpected parts of our bodies, including our brains. Endometriosis. Prolapse. They removed the uterus of my friend. They put children in cages at the border. We were angry at the lie of Women's Lib and Civil Rights, at the failed experiment of our country. We admitted to ourselves that white people could not be redeemed. We were taunted by our president's tweets. Unsure what to do with our rage, we turned it on ourselves.

Our immune systems attacked us. We grew tumors. "Me, too," we said. "Me too." The previous season we'd been saying "Black Lives Matter." Nobody listened. Nobody knew how to balance our hormones. Probably there was not enough money in it. They theorized it was because we were not bearing enough children. We begged for estrogen and were refused. Our perception was either extremely distorted or crystal clear. Our cells multiplied, rampantly, into more tumors. They tried to remove the breasts of my friend, who insisted on keeping them for the sake of her sex appeal, for the sake of her self and her love of sex, and somehow I understood her stance was rooted in her being African. As for the rest of us, unless we were queer, we were having disappointing sex, or torrid self-destructive love affairs, or no sex at all.

When my senior colleague asked me to wear the pair of fancy lace panties he'd brought back from Paris at the next faculty meeting, I could have reported him. Maybe I should have. But I did not trust the system to take him down. Instead I kept the panties, and waited. They were as multicolored as a peacock feather. They were worthy of Josephine

Baker. They were the sexiest panties I've ever owned. Wearing them was a misdemeanor of survival.

During the hearing of the scoundrel accused of sexual assault nominated to the Supreme Court, I waited at the hospital in radiology for my turn in the MRI machine. CNN played in the waiting room. Everyone present was in pain and disgust with our president. America didn't listen to the woman. The technician gifted me a pair of earplugs. But it was as loud as a uterus inside that white sarcophagus. The clacking noises sounded nearly human. "Dewey," repeated the voice, nonsensically. "God." "Dot." "Did I?" I was not to move.

This was my second time in an MRI machine. The first was to examine a cystic tumor in my throat, years before. It was blocked anger, unreleased. They cut it out of me and now I wear a scar on my neck that makes me look tough, or victimized, depending on point of view. Back then, I hoped the magnetic field and radio waves generating images of my insides might be rearranging my atoms; that I might come out a different person. Preferably a stronger one. But I did not.

Now, shoved back into the machine, I considered patterns of predation. A cervix. A throat. How much could be forced into those openings. How much shit could be swallowed. I recalled my lover, my predator, once telling me not to move. I would feel more pleasure if I kept still, he said before giving me an STD. "Dewey." "God." "Dot." Some people are triggered by the noise, they'd warned me outside the machine, some people get claustrophobic in there. "Did I?" Push this button if you get scared.

It came as no surprise when I was told that I was among the least qualified of the hundreds of applicants who applied for my position, and that I filled a demographic niche as a Black woman. That I should be grateful. I was the gift of diversity. I was living my ancestors' wildest dreams. Therefore, I should not behave as a diva.

The midwife who caught my children years before tried to teach me a new technique called havening. She had me trigger the trauma, massage my own face with the tips of my fingers, and, hugging myself, do the same to the tops of my arms, replicating a mother's touch; to mother myself. I was to repeat this mantra: "I deserve to feel safe." I wanted it to work but admitted it did not. The trigger is too large, reasoned the midwife, the trigger is patriarchy, and all the babies being born to women in this era will inherit the fight-or-flight response through the umbilical cords of their mothers. Wait and see.

When my colleague became my boss I reminded him of the panties. "Ever since you gave me that gift," I lied, "I've understood I could count on you as a friend." I asked him for something. I don't remember what. Probably I asked him for time to myself. Or an office with a window. Whatever it was, I didn't get it.

The integrative health doctor advised me to quit running. "You're running with cement blocks on your feet," she said. "You have next to no bandwidth. You are like a vessel nearly empty of water. You are not strong enough to run." After mixing these metaphors, she gave me the card of a somatic therapist. I recognized the name on the card as belonging to a man who fucked my friend when she sought his help to get her head correct. I asked to see a woman and stopped training for races.

The female somatic therapist told me it was epigenetics causing my pain. The inherited trauma of my enslaved ancestors, the burdens of my grandmother after they lynched my grandfather, etc.… According to the latest study, these injustices were encoded within me. She handed me a foam sledgehammer and encouraged me to use it to externalize my rage. This exercise embarrassed me but I did not wish to hurt the well-meaning white woman's feelings. Performing my rage for her by pounding that silly prop against a loveseat from West Elm, I felt enraged.

The burly physiatrist was so aggressively rude to his cowering receptionist that I walked out of his practice before he could look at my body. I presumed that at home he beat his wife. The gold chain nestled in the black chest hair in the V-neck of his scrubs made me sick.

Patterns of predation were getting amplified in the sloppy court of public opinion. The hunt for a cure was growing expensive. The diagnosis was inexact. My freedom of movement, that is, my range of motion was restricted. This much I knew: I could not afford a broken back. Too many people depended upon me.

The osteopath was a good witch, I could tell. Her fingers felt nice at the base of my skull and I did not exactly think her racist when she theorized that so many Black women in America are overweight because inherited trauma has made us warehouse our fat for the lean times. But by the time I left her padded table for the Korean market next to her practice to buy a pack of frozen black bean buns, my back was hurting again, the weight of it all was too much to bear, her juju was gone.

"You are not symmetrical," the acupuncturist said. "Your muscles are calcified already. Your spine is no good. Your neck is no good. Your psoas is weak." He said he could treat the pain, ninety percent of which was in my head. I believed him ninety percent. Two times a week he needled me with insults. I pondered my pain and tried to breathe. That I could not relax or release was my fault, that my muscles were in constant spasm, that my back had become a carapace, a shield, was my fault. The doctor promised, quite arrogantly, to make the pain go away. On his wall hung a cartoon caricature of the doctor next to a frightened-looking porcupine who asks, "How many needles?"

A log of misalignment when the figure in question intrudes upon my thoughts:

> as I lay upon the acupuncture table
> as I wait for the train
> as I bathe with lavender soap
> as I fall asleep
> as I plank
> as I prolong getting out of bed in the morning
> as I lay out the children's school clothes
> as I peel the green apples
> as I comb my hair before the mirror
> as I photograph birds
> as I move the wet clothes from the washer to the dryer
> as the abuser is confirmed to high office
> as I breathe
> as I attempt to write the novel
> as I wait for the children's school bus
> as I fold the laundry into separate piles

The highest spinal center is located in the medulla oblongata, at the base of the brain just above the place where the neck connects with the skull—the sixth chakra, through which cosmic energy nourishes the body with prana, conscious cosmic energy. I was the only Black woman in the yoga studio where the instructor spoke of chakras as the seven gates of freedom along the astral spine, after asking us to chant *om*, and I didn't forget it, that I was the only Black woman, for the entire class, not even in tree pose where I balanced as straight as I could with a misaligned spine.

Death by a million microaggressions. By air pollution. By disillusionment and the disintegration of kinship structures. By 'The Man.' By the world of goddamned men. By the weight of my grandmother's sorrow. By America. Death by the wolf of debt. A slow, inglorious death.

In the bestselling book on mind-body connection and healing back pain without drugs, surgery, or exercise, the author advises spending fifteen minutes every day reminding the brain that there is no structural problem, in a meditative state meant to induce myofascial release. Knowing that repressed anger and anxiety are the triggers, I am supposed to tell myself my back is fine. And yet,

the structural problem is real.

Nation of Poets

I woke up to a light of sky
and you were my homeland.
When did this happen? How?
I turned my hands in the new
earth of you, because you were
there, in my bed, a mountain
rising. My hands, too—earth
I know and am also made of.
I called you into yourself:
Come, mountain, I said, lifting.
I drank you, river who is
outside wetting my ankles
and also inside running me—
a thick ambering sweet. I am
the river and you are you—
river, carving into the clay
I am carved from. How land is
made is how you became mine.
I want to offer you something
equal, and beauty concerns me
not. Maybe I will become yours—
we call that Nation. I arrived

with a war horse already
foaming in my mind; I come
with bullets glinting feelings
or memories—sometimes they
are the same: bullet, feeling,
memory. Ghosts I try to shoot
except I wear a ghost shirt—I am
singing a _______ ghost song,
except I've already been shot.
I want to shoot the president
of the club but I don't have
a gun—I know what it's like
to pretend to think with one
kissing your temple. It feels
like a meteor leaning into
your mind. The way it feels
when you sink your hand into
a warm lake at night. Instead
of buying a gun, I buy tennis
shoes—air force ones, new,
which are remade versions of
the old ones, except more $.
I have problems: one isn't
ninety-nine. We poets are
failing. We writers. We are
singing for the same post-
reading supper. We are
standing in front of one-
hundred plastic tanks on
the clean streets of Twitter.
We try to pray but only clap—

this is the evolution of *Poetry.*
The tongues left us for bigger
muscles. We remember them,
tongues, because the seals re-
mind us—those thick priests of
the coast praising the tube sock
shape of each other's body,
lying on the warm flat rocks,
like slugs in all the pictures.
Like words. All beautiful, all
took the top of my head off.
All brilliant. And it is—when
light hits water it is brilliant.
Literally. The vultures are also
pretty—they smell us miles away.
We smell like North America,
and we are meaning to write
poems in the sky—meaning
we are circling our lives. We are
in helicopters, live-streaming,
pointing down at the survivors.
We drop them a thousand poems
we wrote overnight. That's how
good we are, so fast. The seals
applaud! What is freedom?
My friend says: *That's not*
freedom, that's just running
around bumping into shit. From
our planes, we can't see that
what else is floating down there,
collapsing down there is our

language. What is a poet with
a line that stopped moving? No
I didn't ask *whose* line stopped
working. I am from the desert—
I am not afraid of shade. Some-
times it is the truth about a tree.
Sometimes it will save you from
vultures licking your bones clean.
Isn't the line the body, wrought
again or again? Or is the line
a pallbearer? Must we carry
our own caskets? The editors,
our senators, are in on it,
thinning our ranks. Hooking us,
on the opioid of trauma.
Traumatizing our language.
Is this linked to the CIA?
Seed-IA. We can be dangerous.
Which is why they won't let us
write good sentences anymore.
Find me a good sentence
and I'll find you someone
who will fight hard in the war.
Don't assume I mean everyone
but me. There is always a donkey
hidden in the scrub brush of
my poems, and the donkey's
name is rigor mortis. I brought
nothing for the children because
they were only wounds,
and still without easy decoration.

I brought nothing for the children
because you asked me to bring it.
It's not easy to tie ribbons to
the chain links. It is not easy
to watch what happened to you
four hundred years ago, or
what is happening to you now
for seven hundred years straight.
I woke up this morning, and
my beloved has become mine
homeland. Meaning I have dis-
placed her with my displacement.
I married her, reader. Invaded her
like any good Nation should.
And then, like any lazy poet,
I wrote a poem about it.

Contributors

Cathy Linh Che is the author of *Split*, winner of the Kundiman Poetry Prize, the Norma Farber First Book Award from the Poetry Society of America, and the Best Poetry Book Award from the Association of Asian American Studies. Her work has been published in *The New Republic*, *Los Angeles Review of Books*, and *Poetry*. She serves as Executive Director at Kundiman and lives in Queens.

Angie Cruz is a novelist and editor. Her novel, *Dominicana* is the inaugural book pick for GMA book club and chosen as the 2019/2020 Wordup Uptown Reads. It was shortlisted for The Women's Prize, longlisted for the Andrew Carnegie Medals for Excellence in Fiction, The Aspen Words Literary Prize, a RUSA Notable book and the winner of the ALA/YALSA Alex Award in fiction. She's an Associate professor at University of Pittsburgh where she teaches in the MFA program and splits her time between Pittsburgh, New York, and Turin.

Natalie Diaz was born and raised in the Fort Mojave Indian Village in Needles, California, on the banks of the Colorado River. She is Mojave and an enrolled member of the Gila River Indian Tribe. Her first poetry collection, *When My Brother Was an Aztec*, was published by Copper Canyon Press in 2012. She is 2018 MacArthur Foundation Fellow, a Lannan Literary Fellow and a Native Arts Council Foundation Artist

Fellow. Diaz teaches at the Arizona State University Creative Writing MFA program.

Ru Freeman is a Sri Lankan born writer and activist whose creative and political work has appeared in the *UK Guardian*, *The Boston Globe*, and the *New York Times*. She is the author of the short story collection, *Sleeping Alone* (forthcoming from Graywolf Press, Spring 2022), and the novels *A Disobedient Girl*, and *On Sal Mal Lane*, a NYT Editor's Choice Book. She is editor of the anthology, *Extraordinary Rendition: (American) Writers on Palestine*, and *Indivisible: Global Leaders on Shared Security*. She is the 2014 winner of the Janet Heidinger Kafka Prize for Fiction by an American Woman. She writes for the Huffington Post on books and politics.

Sarah Gambito is the author of the poetry collections *Loves You* (Persea Books), *Delivered* (Persea Books) and *Matadora* (Alice James Books). Her poems have appeared or are forthcoming in *The Iowa Review*, *POETRY*, *Harvard Review*, *American Poetry Review*, *The New Republic* and other journals. She is Professor of English / Director of Creative Writing at Fordham University and co-founder of Kundiman, a non-profit organization serving writers and readers of Asian American literature and Kindred, an Accelerator for BIPOC artists.

Cristina García is the author of seven novels, including: *Dreaming in Cuban*, *The Agüero Sisters*, *Monkey Hunting*, *A Handbook to Luck*, *The Lady Matador's Hotel*, *King of Cuba*, *Here in Berlin*. García has edited two anthologies, *Cubanísimo: The Vintage Book of Contemporary Cuban Literature* and *Bordering Fires: The Vintage Book of Contemporary Mexican and Chicano/a Literature*. García's work has been nominated for a National Book Award and translated into fourteen languages. She lives in the San Francisco Bay area.

Jamey Hatley is a Memphian obsessed with stories in ruin, at the very edge of being forgotten. Her writing has appeared in the *Oxford American*, *Memphis Noir*, *Strange Horizons*, and elsewhere. She was a Prose Fellow for the National Endowment for the Arts, a Rona Jaffe Foundation Writers' Award Winner, and the inaugural Indie Memphis Black Screenwriting Fellow (selected by Barry Jenkins). Ms. Hatley is a member of the Writers Guild of America, East.

Dawn Lundy Martin is the author of four books of poems: *Good Stock Strange Blood*, winner of the 2019 Kingsley Tufts Award for Poetry; *Life in a Box is a Pretty Life*, which won the Lambda Literary Award for Lesbian Poetry; *DISCIPLINE*, and *A Gathering of Matter / A Matter of Gathering*. Her nonfiction can be found in *n+1*, *The New Yorker*, and *Best American Essays 2019*. Martin is the Toi Derricotte Endowed Chair of African American Poetry at the University of Pittsburgh and Director of the Center for African American Poetry and Poetics.

Ayana Mathis is a graduate of the Iowa Writers' Workshop and a recipient of the 2014-15 New York Public Library's Cullman Center Fellowship. *The Twelve Tribes of Hattie*, her first novel, was a New York Times Bestseller, a 2013 New York Times Notable Book of the Year, an NPR Best Books of 2013, and was chosen by Oprah Winfrey as the second selection for Oprah's Book Club 2.0.

Vi Khi Nao is the author of *Sheep Machine* (Black Sun Lit, 2018) and *Umbilical Hospital* (Press 1913, 2017), and of the short stories collection, *A Brief Alphabet of Torture*, which won FC2's Ronald Sukenick Innovative Fiction Prize in 2016, the novel, *Fish in Exile* (Coffee House Press, 2016), and the poetry collection, *The Old Philosopher*, which won the Nightboat Books Prize for Poetry in 2014. Her work includes poetry, fiction, film and cross-genre collaboration.

Aimee Nezhukumatathil is the author of the Kirkus Prize finalist *World of Wonders: In Praise of Fireflies, Whale Sharks, & Other Astonishments* and four previous poetry collections: *Oceanic, Lucky Fish, At the Drive-In Volcano* and *Miracle Fruit.* Her most recent chapbook is *Lace & Pyrite*, a collaboration of garden poems with the poet Ross Gay. Her writing appears in the *Best American Poetry* Series, *New York Times Magazine, ESPN, Ploughshares,* and *Tin House.* She is professor of English and Creative Writing in the University of Mississippi's MFA program.

Deborah Paredez is the author of the award-winning critical study, *Selenidad: Selena, Latinos, and the Performance of Memory* and of the poetry collections, *This Side of Skin* and *Year of the Dog.* Her poetry and essays have appeared in the *New York Times, Los Angeles Review of Books, National Public Radio, Boston Review, Poetry, Feminist Studies.* She currently lives in New York City where she is a professor of creative writing and ethnic studies at Columbia University and the Co-Founder of CantoMundo, a national organization for Latinx poets.

Khadijah Queen, PhD, is the author of six books, including *I'm So Fine: A List of Famous Men & What I Had On.* Her verse play *Non-Sequitur* won the Leslie Scalapino Award for Innovative Women's Performance Writing. In 2019 she co-edited an op-ed on poetry and disability with Jillian Weise for the *New York Times.* She is an Assistant Professor of creative writing at University of Colorado, Boulder, and serves as core faculty for the Mile-High MFA in creative writing at Regis University. Her sixth book is *Anodyne.*

Emily Raboteau is the author *The Professor's Daughter* and *Searching for Zion*—named a best book of 2013 by The Huffington Post and *The San*

Francisco Chronicle, a finalist for the Hurston Wright Legacy Award, grand prize winner of the New York Book Festival, and winner of a 2014 American Book Award. Her fiction and essays have been widely published and anthologized in *Best American Short Stories*, the *New York Times*, the *New Yorker*, and elsewhere. Raboteau teaches in Harlem at City College, once known as "the poor man's Harvard."

Paisley Rekdal is the author of a book of essays, *The Night My Mother Met Bruce Lee*; the hybrid photo-text memoir, *Intimate*; and six books of poetry: *A Crash of Rhinos*; *Six Girls Without Pants*; *The Invention of the Kaleidoscope*; *Animal Eye*, *Imaginary Vessels* and *Nightingale*. Her newest work of nonfiction is a book-length essay, *The Broken Country: On Trauma, a Crime, and the Continuing Legacy of Vietnam. Appropriate: A Provocation*, which examines cultural appropriation, is forthcoming from W.W. Norton in Feb. 2021.

Lyrae Van Clief-Stefanon is the author of *Open Interval*, a 2009 National Book Award finalist, and *Black Swan*, winner of the 2001 Cave Canem Poetry Prize, as well as *Poems in Conversation and a Conversation*, a chapbook collaboration with Elizabeth Alexander. She is currently at work on *The Coal Tar Colors*, her third poetry collection, and *Purchase*, a collection of essays. She was one of ten celebrated poets commissioned to write poems inspired by Jacob Lawrence's Migration Series in conjunction with the 2015 exhibit One-Way Ticket: Jacob Lawrence's Migration Series and Other Works for MoMA.

Acknowledgments

"Notes on Writing about Sexual Violence" appeared in *AGNI* on May 11, 2020. https://agnionline.bu.edu/blog/notes-on-writing-about-sexual-violence

"Spinal Column" appeared in *Gay Magazine* on February 20, 2020. https://gay.medium.com/spinal-column-12800894f606

"The Patient Records" appeared in *The Point Magazine* on March 25, 2020. https://thepointmag.com/literature/the-patient-records/

Thank you to Caroline Bleeke for editorial support.